OCCUPY!
A Short History of Work

Dave Sherry

OCCUPY!

A SHORT HISTORY OF WORKERS' OCCUPATIONS

Dave Sherry

Bookmarks Publications

Occupy! A Short History of Workers' Occupations
Dave Sherry

First published in February 2010 by Bookmarks Publications
c/o 1 Bloomsbury Street, London WC1B 3QE

Cover photograph: Strike at Citröen, Paris, 1938, by Willy Ronis
Typeset by Bookmarks Publications
Printed by Melita Press Malta

ISBN 978 1905 192 625

CONTENTS

1.

THE PRESENT IS HISTORY

THE COLLAPSE of Lehmann Brothers in 2008 triggered the biggest financial crash since 1929 and pushed the world economy into its deepest crisis since the 1930s. Despite all the recent talk of recovery the crisis is far from over. In November 2009 the Gulf city state of Dubai became its latest casualty.

Bosses worldwide are squeezing workers harder and harder. Over the last 18 months a third more jobs have been lost in the US than had been predicted by the economic experts. Everywhere you look, factories, offices, banks and retail stores are closing down.

The National Institute for Social and Economic Research estimates that Britain's gross domestic product (GDP) fell by 4.8 percent in 2009. This is Britain's biggest annual economic contraction since 1921. UK unemployment now stands at 2.5 million. Young people are particularly hard hit: among under-25s the jobless figure has jumped by nearly 250,000 since 2008. At 18 percent, the unemployment rate for 18 to 24 year olds is the highest since records began in 1992.

Gordon Brown promised to create "a million green jobs". So why did his government allow the bosses at Vestas to close Britain's only significant wind turbine plant and sack another 600 people? No wonder so many young people feel alienated, or older workers, who fear for their jobs, their homes and their pensions, feel so bitter about government bail-outs for the bankers.

The Bank of England estimates that public funding used to bail out the banks in the US, the UK and the

Eurozone during the current crisis totals a staggering $14 trillion, or almost a quarter of global GDP, dwarfing any previous state support of the banking system. Yet despite this, the recovery is extremely feeble and fragile.

Some financial experts anticipate a period of stagnation, while others warn of "a double-dip recession", and forecast further losses for British banks over the next two years of up to £250 billion. Meanwhile, the vast government sums used to avert the complete collapse of the financial system will have to be recouped.

We have been here before: for Gordon Brown read Ramsay McDonald, darling of the Labour left, leader of the 1929 Labour cabinet that slashed wages, dole money and public spending, yet still couldn't satisfy the bankers' demands for cuts. In 1931 McDonald deserted Labour to form a National Government with the Tories.

In 2000 Tony Cliff, a revolutionary socialist since 1933, warned:

> The story of the 1990s is like a film of the 1930s in slow motion. The defeat of the German working class by Hitler was a catastrophe that cannot be overestimated. But at the same time we had the mass occupation of the factories in France in June 1936 that raised the spectre of revolution. The 1930s was a decade of extremes... The fact that the film of the 1930s returns but in slow motion means there is much greater opportunity to stop the film and direct it in the way we want. The key is building the revolutionary party.

Martin Wolf used the same analogy in the *Financial Times* in March 2008: "There is a whiff of 1929 about all this." No one really knows what will happen next—least of all those who championed the free market ideology that brought us to where we are. But the world slump, the growth of the Nazi BNP and the failure of the left in Britain to get its act together add urgency to

Cliff's warning of a decade ago. The slow motion replay of the 1930s is speeding up.

Encouragingly, we are witnessing the return of a militant form of collective action associated with some of the great, mass struggles of the past—a form of action that many thought had vanished along with the 1970s—factory occupations.

2009 began with a wave of student occupations in protest at Israel's assault on Gaza. Then in February workers at Waterford Glass occupied their factory, inspiring the Prisme occupation in Dundee. In April the Belfast Visteon workers occupied when they were sacked and the Enfield Visteon plant went into occupation too. In Glasgow a group of parents occupied Wyndford Primary School to halt its closure by the Labour council.

In August workers at Vestas on the Isle of Wight occupied to save their jobs. Their fight sparked solidarity protests and meetings around the world. Bob Crow of the RMT told the *Guardian*:

> The Vestas occupation and the action at Visteon show workers under attack can develop tactics that drive a coach and horses through the anti-union laws instead of just bending at the knee and accepting their fate.

One of the Vestas occupiers told *Socialist Worker*:

> In the past I didn't believe change could come from workers. But this process has proved to me that if you stand up collectively then you can inspire other people to do the same... Occupations don't happen very often but at times like this they need to spread quickly.

Anyone involved in raising solidarity for these occupations understood their significance, as one activist told *International Socialism*:

The experience bears out all the stories you hear about how people shift in struggle... If you want a dispute which summarises the argument why political trade unionism is a key factor, Vestas is it... It sums up as well the argument about the role of individuals and socialists. If people had just sat back in the traditional way, waiting for something to happen, Vestas would never have erupted. There are lots of situations at the moment where whether people decide to fight or not is on a knife edge. Since the 1970s most people don't have experience of situations where socialists can intervene to such an effect.

The minority in the working class with some level of militancy and consciousness feel more confident now. Saying, "We can fight and here's Visteon, here's Vestas and here's Lindsey [the unofficial strike at the Lindsey oil refinery, which spread to 20 other construction sites and won]", is much easier than simply saying, "We ought to fight." That was the difficulty at Cowley [the sacking of workers on short-term contracts at the Mini car plant in Oxford] at the beginning of the year. There were not those clear examples of what could be done. Were the Cowley sackings to happen now, someone would probably say, "We can fight because Visteon and Vestas did."

Hard on the heels of Vestas, London bus workers launched their pay campaign by occupying the foyer of the Transport for London building. Thomas Cook workers in Dublin occupied too.

This was not a list of random incidents; there was a conscious process at work. BBC employment correspondent Martin Shankelman noted:

when faced with challenging the plans of large corporations, it's hardly surprising that a growing number of workers see sit-ins as the most direct and effective way of registering their protests. It is likely we should expect more.

This short history of workplace occupations is written to encourage more occupations and to show that when workers act in this way they begin to sense their collective capacity, not just to win local battles, but to challenge the system and change the world.

Protesters brought down the Icelandic government in January 2009.

2.

RECESSION AND RESISTANCE

"The spectre of 1968 is haunting Europe."
—French president Sarkozy, February 2009

ACROSS EUROPE the onset of recession provoked an immediate response from below. In France there was a general strike. There were also mass strikes in Spain, Greece, Italy and Ireland and big protests against austerity measures in Latvia, Russia and Iceland.

Here in Britain workers' initial response was muted and slow by comparison. Years of defeat had sapped workers' confidence. But in 2009 we saw growing resistance. Occupations and a series of successful "wildcat" strikes showed more and more groups of workers were ready to go beyond the union leaders and break from the pessimism that was so prevalent after the big defeats of the 1980s and 1990s.

This does not mean our side has broken through and that everything is on the up. There are far too many places where redundancies go ahead unchallenged. In Redcar there was a big demonstration over sackings at the Corus steel plant but there was no fight.

At the Johnnie Walker whisky plant in Kilmarnock 20,000 people—half the town's population—marched against job losses and plant closure. Industrial action to save the jobs would have been hugely popular and would have embarrassed the giant multinational Diageo. Yet four months elapsed between that great march in Kilmarnock and the union leaders organising a "consultative" ballot for industrial action, which although it forced the company to offer better redundancy terms, failed to save the jobs.

There is a battle between the old and the new—between the militant character of the new resistance and the old bureaucratic inertia of the union leaders and their links to Labour. The outcome of last November's postal strike shows how the old can hold back the new but it also saw the labour government and the Royal Mail bosses back off from an all-out confrontation with the most militant group of workers in Britain.

We are constantly told that resistance is futile because globalisation means workers in Britain, or anywhere else, cannot stand up to the multinationals. Too often our union leaders accept this. But the opposite is true. When Ford workers in Britain struck in 1988 they brought the whole of Ford Europe to a halt in three days.

The technological and organisational changes of the past 20 years can operate to workers' advantage. During the 1980s the world's car firms adopted the Japanese "just in time" system of keeping very low stocks of parts.

In 1994 12,000 workers at General Motors' Flint, Michigan, complex went on strike against GM's policy of increasing overtime rather than hiring new workers to meet increasing demand. GM laid off 20,000 workers as their plants in Europe ran out of parts. After three days the company caved in and agreed to hire 800 new workers. Similarly when 3,000 General Motors workers went on strike in Dayton, Ohio, in 1996 they shut down GM across the US, Canada and Mexico. GM laid off 125,000 workers and the strike cost the company $50 million a day.

Recent events prove once again that workers can win. Visteon was hived-off by Ford and then outsourced. At the end of March, Ford UK told the *Financial Times* that, "it was not in a position to fund insolvent suppliers".

But when three Visteon plants occupied and workers threatened to picket Ford's profitable Bridgend plant, Ford UK intervened to make sure Visteon—"the insolvent supplier"—could hand over £20 million to its former workers. Multinationals are vulnerable and industrial action can have a bigger impact than ever before.

Here in Britain, despite a sharp rise in unemployment, 2009 was marked by a significant increase in militancy: the occupations at Waterford Glass, Prisme Dundee, Visteon and Vestas; the successful wildcat walkouts in the construction industry; the all-out strikes that saved jobs and conditions at Leeds bins and at Tower Hamlets College; and the postal strikes before Christmas. 2010 opened with the prospect of a renewed fight at British Airways and a national strike ballot across the civil service.

Resistance matters. In any crisis someone is going to pay. Those who created the mess we are in want it to be us. The efforts of the ruling class to shift the cost of the crisis onto working people by severe cuts in public spending, jobs, wages and pensions will shape the coming period.

Whoever wins the next UK general election will be forced to launch the most savage onslaught on working people since the Second World War. Martin Wolf of the *Financial Times* has already spelt out what this will mean:

> a sustained freeze...decentralised pay bargaining, employee contributions to public pensions and a pruning of benefits... The next prime minister is likely to end up as hated as Margaret Thatcher was. [25 May 2009]

Economic growth in 2010/11 is likely to be 10 percent lower than the Treasury predicted in 2007. Labour chancellor Alastair Darling has announced 14 percent real cuts in public spending over 2011-14. The rate of job losses in the public sector has accelerated sharply in recent months.

Millions know New Labour puts the interests of the rich and powerful before everyone else. No wonder postal workers in London voted by a massive 96 percent to suspend CWU union funding of New Labour. The fight against the privatisation of Royal Mail is crucial for every worker, student, pensioner and unemployed person in Britain.

The Confederation of British Industry is demanding a 50 percent increase in student fees and a rise in student loan interest payments. It backs the business-driven media campaign to convince us that the postal service can only survive if it is privatised; that public sector workers will have to accept pay and pension cuts as well as job losses; and that those lucky enough to have a job will have to work longer and harder.

Yet their side has big problems. While some sections of the ruling class are howling for cuts, the *Financial Times* has been expressing ruling class anxiety: "Financiers are back to their high-earning ways, while tens of millions of people have lost their jobs...little wonder bonus-bashing is on the menu."

Workers are asking why they should pay for the greed and incompetence of the bankers, and recent polls show 50 percent of those surveyed think all MPs are corrupt. The long-running Westminster expenses scandal makes it difficult for any politician to call for working class sacrifice and keep a straight face. But the pressure on working people is going to intensify and it will not ease until there is a general counter-offensive from our side.

Capitalism and chaos

If life for workers in Britain is going to get tougher, it will be catastrophic for the poor in Africa, Asia and

Latin America. Capitalism is a system driven by profit and competition; it cannot serve the people of the world. Not enough food and medicines are produced because it isn't profitable to produce them in sufficient quantities. Workers are unemployed because it isn't profitable to give them a job.

There is a fundamental conflict between the livelihoods and welfare of most people on this planet and the profits of a tiny handful. The Haitian earthquake is the latest indictment of a system locked into economic chaos and permanent war. If capitalism is allowed to continue much longer it will starve billions to death and disfigure and destroy the planet—either through ecological catastrophe or nuclear war or both.

If humanity is to survive and prosper we will need to get rid of capitalism. But can workers make that leap? Will they resist in large enough numbers? And can they win?

Some people argue that the fear of job losses will stop workers from fighting back, that economic slump destroys any hope of class struggle. But this ignores the fact that some of the most inspirational workers' struggles have taken place during economic recession. The 1930s saw the biggest slump the world had ever seen. But it was also a decade of militancy as across the globe workers took part in mass strikes, mutinies and revolutions.

There is no automatic link between recession and rising class struggle. Mass unemployment doesn't automatically mean workers will become more political or even more militant. It can breed fear, division and despair.

Russian revolutionary Leon Trotsky argued that workers' willingness to mount collective resistance is shaped to a large extent by the material conditions they face. A spark falling on wet grass is unlikely to start a fire but dry tinder is more combustible. In the 1920s Trotsky insisted, "There is no automatic dependence of the revolutionary movement upon a crisis." He went on to make a number of valuable points about the relationship between recession and resistance:

> The political effects of a crisis are determined by the entire existing political situation and by those events which precede and accompany the crisis, especially the battles, successes or failures of the working class itself prior to the crisis. Under one set of conditions the crisis may give a mighty impulse to the revolutionary activity of the working masses; under a different set of circumstances it may completely paralyse the offensive of the proletariat.

He also pointed out that while the onset of crisis could demoralise workers, the underlying bitterness it created would persist and could spark an explosion when the opportunity for united action presented itself:

> On the basis of this economic depression the bourgeoisie will be compelled to exert stronger and stronger pressure on the working class. This is already seen in the cutting of wages... It might be asked whether these great struggles over wages, a classic example of which is the miners' strike in England, will lead automatically to world revolution, to the final civil war and the struggle for the conquest of political power. However, it is not Marxist to pose the question in such a way...
>
> Many comrades say that if an improvement takes place in this epoch it would be fatal for our revolution. No, under no circumstances... Let us look at Russia. The 1905 Revolution was defeated and the workers bore great sacrifices. Throughout 1907-1909 the most terrible crisis reigned. It killed the movement completely because the workers had suffered so greatly during the struggle that the

depression could act only to dishearten them. Between 1910 and 1912 there was an improvement in our economic situation, which acted to reassemble the demoralised workers who had lost their courage. They realised again how important they were in production and they passed over to the offensive, first in the economic field and later in the political field too. On the eve of the war the working class had become so consolidated, thanks to this period of prosperity, that it was able to pass to a direct assault.

We are on the eve of a period of depression and this is incontestable. With such a perspective, a mitigation of the crisis would not signify a mortal blow to the revolution but would enable the working class to gain a breathing spell during which it could undertake to reorganise its ranks in order subsequently to pass over to the attack on a firmer basis. [*The First Five Years of the Communist International*, vol 1]

It is important to understand that economic crisis is a protracted process, not a single event. This is especially true of the current recession, which will continue to dominate politics but won't unfold on a steady, predictable, upward curve. There will be transitory upswings and downswings, ebbs and flows, recoveries and setbacks.

It is also important to grasp the depth and severity of the present crisis. It is a *world* crisis and compels our ruling class to launch a ferocious attack that most of us have never previously experienced. In Britain inflation meant that real wages had been declining even before the recession arrived. For many workers the promise of prosperity in the boom years had been based on rising house prices and expanding debt. Now the bubble has burst, the system stands exposed in the eyes of millions.

Workers enter this recession after three decades of privatisation, deregulation and anti-union laws. The latest crisis proves that capitalism doesn't work but it is not the first or only such proof. There is a deep cynicism about the political system in general and massive disenchantment with a Labour Party wedded to the free market. All of this comes on the back of the radicalisation created by the rise of the anti-capitalist and anti-war movements in the first half of the decade.

The modest yet significant revival of industrial struggle and the return of militant action in the form of occupations, unofficial "wild cat" strikes and all out action have to be seen in this context. At a certain stage the anger, frustration and bitterness that have accumulated over the last decade could burst to the surface in a wave of militancy not seen for over 30 years.

That's precisely what happened in the 1930s. When the stock market crashed spectacularly in 1929, the sharp, sudden crisis and the insecurity of mass unemployment weakened workers' confidence. It was only after five years, when the crisis eased slightly in 1934, that the resistance exploded in the US, and then in France and Spain. In Britain trade union organisation only recovered during the build up of rearmament for the Second World War.

It might be economic factors which trigger militancy. A modest recovery that sees the rate of unemployment slow and workers stop being sacked can create confidence and lead to widespread industrial action. In America in 1934 a mild industrial recovery provoked a wave of bitter strikes and sit-downs, which led to the mass unionisation of industry, huge material and cultural gains for the working class and the growth of the far left.

Political crisis

It could be a political crisis that sets things alight. France had been through ten years of austerity, right wing repression and falling living standards when Parisian students battled with the French riot cops in May 1968. Within days, 10 million workers were taking part in the biggest general strike in history, and large swathes of the French economy were occupied under workers' control. Out of this explosion a new left was born.

Mass resistance can occur when our rulers go too far. The Heath Tory government of 1970 was elected on the most right wing manifesto since the 1930s. Using rising unemployment, tough wage controls, and draconian anti-union laws, it launched a vicious assault on workers. It provoked a series of militant strikes and occupations: the work-in at Upper Clyde Shipbuilders in 1971 that inspired a wave of over 200 occupations; the mass picketing that characterised the mining, docks and builders' strikes of 1972; and the second miners' strike of 1974.

More than 3 million days were "lost" in political protest strikes against the Industrial Relations Act and more than 1.5 million against the government's incomes policy. Militant trade unionism smashed the anti-union laws and freed the Pentonville dockers who had been jailed for defying them. In the winter of 1973-74 severe power cuts and the introduction of the three-day week resulting from the miners' national overtime ban and their subsequent strike put the lights out on the Tories and finally forced them from office.

None of this would have happened without socialist politics. There were maybe 20,000 union activists who were members or close supporters of the Communist Party and another 5,000 who were members of the revolutionary left. Together these made up only a small minority of union activists—perhaps 25,000 out of a total of 300,000. But their independence from the Labour Party meant they could push struggles beyond the limits laid down by the trade union and labour leaders.

It's not always the best organised or the biggest battalions who become the vanguard. One of the most effective strikes in recent years occurred when 500 British Airways check-in staff, mostly women, walked out on unofficial strike and shut down Heathrow Airport. Inspiration can come from the least experienced or from groups of workers with no tradition of struggle or organisation.

This is how the New Unionism of the 1880s and 1890s was born. Before then only 10 percent of the working class were in trade unions. The conservative, male-dominated, craft unions that had grown in the previous three decades were incapable of defending and organising the mass of the new unskilled and semi-skilled workers.

The revolt of the unskilled, women and migrant workers was spearheaded by the Bryant & May match girls' strike of 1888. Led by teenage women, many of them immigrants from Ireland, their victory heralded the great dock strike and the formation of powerful general unions which called for a fundamental change in society.

The upsurge of the New Unionism depended on the involvement and leadership of socialist activists like Annie Besant, Eleanor Marx and Tom Mann. And the rise of the movement led to the growth of socialist ideas and organisation.

Socialists have always been at the heart of any working class revival. Revolutionary socialists like Willie Gallagher and J T Murphy were crucial in the building of the first shop stewards movements in Glasgow and Sheffield.

The Communist Party led the struggle to build strong workplace organisation in the car plants, the aircraft industry and light engineering in the 1930s. In the 1970s the International Socialists, forerunners of the

SWP, helped launch a vibrant rank and file movement. Today the success of any working class revival will depend on how socialists relate to the struggles that are happening now.

The Vestas occupation became a cause celebre in the summer of 2009.
(Photograph by Tim Dalinian Jones london.indymedia.org)

3.

STANDING UP TO THE BOSSES BY SITTING IN

> The sit-in at the Isle of Wight wind turbine plant was the latest in Britain and part of a wider trend of militant tactics being used as far afield as the US, South Korea and China... In France where such tactics have been more common, the manager of a British company was taken hostage by workers today in a dispute over redundancies—the latest case of so-called "boss-napping" in France.
> —*Guardian*, 24 July 2009

THE TRADE union activists' magazine *Labour Research*, tells the same story. An article headed "Workplace Occupations—What do we Have to Lose?" (August 2009), explains the outcome of recent Irish and UK occupations and reports on other successful sit-ins around the world:

> "A truly astounding victory" is how Kevin Nolan, Unite convenor at the Visteon factory in Enfield, described the outcome... But Nolan and his Visteon colleagues are not the only ones who have taken over their workplace recently...
>
> Workers have occupied a number of factories in Argentina... There have been a string of occupations in the US and Canada. The best known is Republic Windows & Doors in Chicago... The occupiers received huge support, with the Reverend Jesse Jackson describing the occupation as "the beginning of a larger movement for mass action to resist economic violence". The workers won holiday and

severance pay and the company opened under new ownership with some jobs saved...

In February this year 2,300 workers occupied Ukraine's Kherson heavy vehicle manufacturing plant... That same month 3,000 workers staged a sit-in at the Adrama textiles factory in Egypt over bonus payments. There had previously been similar action in 2008 at the country's Sammanoud textile plant, when 1,300 workers occupied to insist their food allowance was doubled...

In France workers at Goss International in Nantes, which makes newspaper printing machines, occupied their factory to prevent its closure. After five days they received assurances that parts of the plant would be retained and most jobs would be saved.

There have been occupations in a number of factories in Turkey including Meha Textile, while in May thousands of workers at Ssangyon, one of the biggest car plants in South Korea, occupied the company's factory in protest at lay-offs.

And despite their country's repressive regime, workers in China have also taken direct action. At a Shanghai computer factory 1,000 workers staged a sit-in in December. Not long after, workers in Guangzhou followed suit by occupying their factory.

Probably the most famous of all UK occupations in the last half century was the 1971-72 occupation of Upper Clyde Shipbuilders (UCS), the largest of around 200 occupations in the early 1970s... From the mid-1970s there was a marked decline in this form of struggle, although sit-ins, such as at Lee Jeans in Greenock in 1981 and the 1996 Glasgow Glacier engineering factory sit-in, kept the flame of occupation burning.

Why occupation makes sense

Sit-ins and occupations have primarily been used to fight closures, lay-offs and sackings. It is still a very effective method of beating back bosses and winning major concessions.

Occupations inspire other groups of workers, and when they spread, the struggle can quickly shift from a defensive local fight to a wider offensive against the employers and the government. Successful occupations extend the frontier of working class control and raise the general level of workers' self-activity. They can quickly alter the balance of power between capital and labour.

The global recession of 2000-01 ravaged Argentina, a state that had made one of the sharpest turns towards neoliberalism. In December 2001 there was a currency devaluation and a run on the banks. With factories closing and unemployment soaring over 20 percent, working people decided they were no longer willing to pay for a crisis caused by their rulers. Unemployed pickets blocked the highways and hundreds of workplaces were taken over by their workers.

It was part of an uprising that toppled four presidents in as many weeks. In his recent book, *Live Working or Die Fighting*, Paul Mason wrote:

> Of the factories occupied during the 2001 upheaval about 160 remain under workers' control. Some are demanding to be nationalised permanently; others want to remain cooperatives, or want government grants to become solvent again under new management.

In 1937 there were 500 sit-down strikes in the US. A key point made by Leon Trotsky during that great struggle is still as relevant now:

> Sit-down strikes go beyond the limits of normal capitalist procedure. Independent of the demands of the strikers, temporary seizure of the factories deals a blow to capitalist

property. Every sit-down poses in a practical manner the question of who is the boss of the factory, the capitalist or the workers?

Occupation has many practical advantages over the traditional forms of strike action. It is often more effective and less risky to take over the workplace than to simply walk out on strike:

* Occupation sweeps aside the anti-union laws and all the obstacles designed to frustrate, delay and block effective strike action.
* It prevents scabbing and stops the bosses locking out those on strike. Bosses are more reluctant to resort to strikebreaking tactics, because workers have control of millions of pounds worth of machinery, company property, raw materials, unfinished work, and data stored on the IT systems.
* Occupation puts bosses on the defensive, making it harder for them to undermine and divide the workforce. Denying management access to the plant prevents the removal of goods and machinery and the delivery of completed work to clients and customers.
* In an occupation the workers' morale is heightened. On the inside they know for certain they have halted production and/or have stopped the closure of the plant. Above all, an occupation challenges the acceptance that the factory belongs to the boss. The workers feel that they are in control.
* The occupied workplace becomes a 24-hour nerve centre that can be used for meetings, activities, entertainment and planning visits to other workplaces. It is warm and dry and provides accommodation and facilities not available on a picket line.
* Occupation allows other workers and groups to deliver solidarity and support. It makes it easier to get

backing from the community. It is also more visible for the media.

* Occupation brings a higher degree of solidarity and militancy. It keeps the strikers together and encourages mass involvement. It means strikers are not isolated at home and it improves communication, cooperation and camaraderie.

* Occupation encourages rank and file initiative and involvement. It means less dependence on union officials.

It is important to act quickly and take over the workplace straight away, particularly when the fight is over sackings. Endless meetings and negotiations merely give management the chance to divide and weaken the resolve of the workforce.

Very few occupations have begun with a formal recommendation to a mass meeting that then agreed to occupy on such and such a date. That only alerts management and gives them time to act. Sit-ins often start from the initiative of a small minority. But this can only work if the initiative seeks and wins the active support of the majority. The occupation has to become the property of the workforce through regular mass meetings.

The strength of an occupation is the ability to control buildings, machinery, materials, equipment and information that the bosses either need to run their business, or that they want to sell or move to other places. The owners or the asset-strippers will prize this stuff, and the more the workers hold onto it, the keener the other side will be to negotiate.

It is also important that occupations look outwards. Don't just occupy. Use the workplace as a base for getting strikers around the movement and the community to win support. Occupation is a powerful weapon but its real potential rests on winning solidarity and spreading the action.

Every shop stewards committee should be discussing plans for occupation now. Each workplace should have a policy which includes occupation to fight redundancies, whether they are in the air or not. That way you can move faster if and when they do arise.

In their book about the wave of strikes and factory occupations that shook France in 1936, *June '36: Class Struggle and the Popular Front in France*, Jacques Danos and Marcel Gibelin made an important point about the law:

> All who have written on this subject have agreed on recognising the illegality of the factory occupations, which are regarded as an attack on the hallowed right of property. We will look no further into this question of legality, recalling only that all the achievements of the working class have involved methods operating either at the margin of the law or in clear opposition to it.

This is an important question because invariably workers engaged in struggle come into conflict with their own union leaders over the question of the law. At Visteon, for example, the union officials used the threat of the law to get workers at the north London plant to end the occupation.

Art Preis, who chronicled the great sit-down strikes in the US during the 1930s in *Labor's Giant Step: Twenty Years of the CIO*, put his finger on the source of this conflict—and socialists have a special responsibility to remember his words today:

> What most disturbed the CIO [Congress of Industrial Organisations] as well as the AFL [American Federation of Labour] union leaders about the sit-downs was the revolutionary implications of the workers' seizure, even temporarily, of the means of production. Union officialdom,

abject servants of the capitalist system, saw in the sit-downs a defiance of the dogma of the sacredness of private property and free enterprise. If workers could seize the plants to enforce their economic demands, why could they not seize them as part of a more far-reaching social programme? Why could they not eliminate the private owners altogether and organise production on the basis of social ownership? Such revolutionary ideas are inherent in the very nature of the sit-down. The workers of America showed themselves far less inclined than their leaders to hold private property in the means of production as sacred. They quickly understood where the heart of the owners' power lay and they put their hand on that heart when they took over his property.

Occupations were virtually unknown in Britain before the UCS work-in began in July 1971. But they have a long pedigree in the international workers' movement. The following chapters focus on some key moments in that rich experience: Italy 1920; France and the US in the 1930s; France 1968; and the experience in Britain since the early 1970s.

A factory occupation in Italy, 1920, during the "two red years".

4.

ITALY 1920: THE OCCUPATION OF THE FACTORIES

> The First World War precipitated an international revolutionary crisis. That the high-point had already occurred in the Bolshevik Revolution of October 1917 was far from apparent during the immediate post-war years. October was widely seen, both on the right and the left, as a beginning, not as an end. Reasonable men could anticipate the Hungarian, Austrian, German, Italian and even the British revolutions. In particular it was the phenomenon of the soviet, of workers' councils, that characterised the international crisis.
>
> —**James Hinton,** ***The First Shop Stewards Movement*** (1973)

"SOVIET" IS the Russian word for "council". The soviet first emerged in St Petersburg during the 1905 Revolution as a council of factory delegates. Formed first as a strike committee by print workers, it developed into a body which represented all the workers of that city. It cut across trade union divisions and based itself on the power of workplace organisation.

The 1905 Revolution was crushed, but the soviets reappeared on a massive scale when the revolution of February 1917 toppled Tsarism. This time the councils covered not only workers, but millions of soldiers who were in revolt against Russia's involvement in the First World War, and peasants fighting the landowners.

The councils created their own workers' militia—the Red Guard. The Provisional Government, which had replaced the Tsar but wanted to continue the war and stabilise Russian capitalism, had to confront what was effectively a workers' government, growing in strength and popularity.

It was a situation of dual power. Either the Russian capitalist class would move to crush the workers' councils or the councils would take power. The workers defeated an attempted counter-revolution. Led by the Bolsheviks, they toppled the Provisional Government in October 1917.

The Russian working class became the first exploited class in history to take and hold power for more than a few weeks. They took control of the factories, offices, transport facilities, banks and government departments. Peasants seized the land they had worked on for generations and kicked out the landlords who had dominated their lives.

The October Revolution was no isolated event. It was part of a wave of workers' militancy which rocked the whole of Europe. In Germany workers', soldiers' and sailors' councils toppled the Kaiser in November 1918, ending the First World War. There were revolutions in Austria and Hungary that overthrew the ruling Hapsburgs. The National Shop Stewards and Workers Committee Movement brought Britain to the brink of revolution in 1919.

The Russian Revolution was greeted enthusiastically by a war-weary European working class, especially in Italy, where the years 1919-20 have come to be known as the "Biennio Rosso"—the two red years. In September 1920 a wave of strikes swept the country. Over half a million workers occupied the factories, set up councils to run them, and reached towards political power. The Italian state seemed on the point of collapse.

The Italian socialist Antonio Gramsci was a key participant in the Turin Factory Council Movement. The councils organised all workers, whether they were in a union or not. Gramsci connected the example of working class power which had emerged in Russia with the experience of workers in other countries:

> We say that the present period is revolutionary precisely because we can see that the working class, in all countries, is tending to generate from within itself, with the utmost vital energy, proletarian institutions of a new type; representative in basis and industrial in arena. We say that the present period is revolutionary because the working class tends with all its energy and all its will power to found its own state.

For Gramsci the soviets were not an artificial institution imported from outside or imposed from above. They grew out of the struggle of workers within the process of production itself, "the product of a real historical situation and an achievement of the working class itself". He saw the Turin workers' councils as the existing working class institutions which could become the bridge to a future socialist society.

The war had been a disaster for Italy. Peasant conscripts were herded into a series of futile battles and slaughtered. 600,000 were killed and 700,000 permanently disabled. In October 1917 the Italian army was routed at Caporetto and the area around Venice was occupied.

War production meant super-exploitation of the workers. The northern cities of Turin, Genoa and Milan formed a great industrial triangle whose workforce swelled as the factories sucked in labour from the countryside as well as huge numbers of women. Giant concerns such as Fiat and Pirelli dominated Italian industry. By the end of the war there were half a million workers in engineering. The workforce at Fiat increased from 7,000 to 30,000.

The industrialists made vast profits, but the impact of the war economy—increasing work discipline and soaring prices—led to food riots and strikes. In Italy, as elsewhere, the metal industry was key. Skilled metal workers became increasingly militant as their conditions were eroded by mechanisation and speed-up.

Turin and the factory councils

In Turin engineering workers became the voice of opposition to the war economy. In August 1917 the city erupted in food riots initiated by working class women, who were expected to queue for hours on end to collect food rations and work a 12-hour day in the factories. The state murdered hundreds of demonstrators and jailed 800. Riots turned into walkouts when the women made the crucial link with workers' industrial power.

Under the influence of Gramsci and the other revolutionaries grouped around the popular newspaper he edited, *L'Ordine Nuovo*, the Turin workers developed independent rank and file organisation based on the internal commissions—Italy's equivalent of shop stewards committees.

L'Ordine Nuovo lifted the Turin movement beyond the narrow confines of trade unionism, and a network of factory councils arose that began to pose the question of workers' power. There was a two-day strike in solidarity with Soviet Russia. In February 1919 the metal workers of Italy won the eight-hour day, and by November 1919 the Turin section of Fiom, the metal workers' union, adopted the principle of factory councils. In the rural south returning ex-soldiers led peasants in occupying the land, and agricultural strikes swept the Po Valley, Veneto, Umbria and Tuscany.

The Italian trade union movement and the Italian Socialist Party (PSI) were in their infancy. The growth of the main union federation, the socialist CGL, was very impressive. At the end of the war it had 250,000 members. Within two years it had grown to 2 million. The PSI increased its membership ten-fold in two years, growing from 23,000 in 1918 to 220,000 by 1920. In the general election of 1919 it received 2 million votes—a third of the total—winning 156 seats and taking control of 2,800 local councils.

Two months earlier the PSI had affiliated to the Communist International and its leaders spoke the language of revolution. But Trotsky, key organiser of the Russian Revolution, noted the gap between words and deeds:

> Everything written in *Avanti* [the socialist newspaper] and everything uttered by the spokesmen of the Socialist Party was taken by the masses as a summons to revolution... But...the Socialist Party conducted a verbally revolutionary policy without ever taking into account any of the consequences.

Those consequences were seen in April 1920, when half a million Turin workers struck in a principled defence of their factory councils. The strike spread throughout the entire region of Piedmont. The state backed the employers and, fearing insurrection, turned Turin into an armed fortress. 50,000 troops were garrisoned in the city and armoured cars roamed the streets.

After a month-long confrontation the Turin workers were defeated, largely because the PSI and the CGL leadership refused to support the strike and spread it. Although the Turin section of the Socialist Party was playing a leading role in the workers' council movement, the leaders of the Socialist Party outside of Turin had solidly opposed it. Gramsci and the leaders of the factory council movement were attacked as "adventurers" by their own party leaders.

But Gramsci pointed out what was at stake and warned of the leadership's passivity:

> The present phase of the class struggle in Italy is the phase that precedes either the conquest of political power by the revolutionary proletariat and the transition to new modes of production and distribution...or a tremendous reaction on the part of the propertied classes and governing caste. No violence will be spared in subjecting the industrial and agricultural proletariat to servile labour... The Socialist Party watches the course of events like a spectator; it never has an opinion of its own to express.

The decisive battle came in September 1920. For months the metal workers had been pursuing a wage rise to catch up with soaring inflation. In August negotiations broke down and the bosses refused any increase. The sacking of militants and the lockout of 2,000 union members at Alfa Romeo in Milan on 31 August provoked the immediate occupation of 300 factories in the Milan area. On 1 September Turin workers swiftly joined the movement, and revolutionaries were central to what developed there. The occupations took on elements of dual power. Armed workers defended the factories and the elected workers' councils began to act like soviets.

Gwyn Williams, in his 1975 book *Proletarian Order*, describes how the movement then developed:

> Between 1 and 4 September metal workers occupied their factories throughout the Italian peninsula. The occupations rolled forward not only in the industrial heartland around Milan, Turin and Genoa but in Rome, Florence, Naples and Palermo, in a forest of red and black flags and a fanfare of workers' bands. Within three days 400,000 workers were in occupation. As the movement spread to

other sectors, the total rose to over half a million. Everyone was stunned by the response.

Within a week the numbers occupying were estimated at 600,000. These were not just occupations over wages. They were a direct challenge to the Italian state. In plant after plant production was restarted under workers' control. The Turin council movement revived and Gramsci was jubilant: "One day like this is worth ten years of normal activity."

The issue of workers' control had been buried under the rubble of the Turin defeat in April. Now it was alive again and everything had changed, as Gramsci wrote in *Avanti* in September 1920:

> When workers struggled to improve their economic condition through a strike, the duty of workers in struggle was limited to a faith in remote leaders, to the building of solidarity and resistance grounded precisely in this generalised faith. But if workers occupy the factories and go on producing, the moral position of the mass abruptly assumes a different form and value. Union bosses can no longer lead. Union bosses dwindle in the immensity of the perspective. The mass must solve the problem of the factory itself, with its own means, its own men.

The movement spread beyond engineering to the wool and cotton mills, to hosiery and textile firms, coal mines, tyre factories, breweries and distilleries, warehouses and tanneries. The ports were closed and ships occupied. Throughout Italy the occupation was total: wherever there was a factory, unionised or not, there was an occupation. Factory councils were established and workers' commissars appointed to maintain transport and supply food and materials. Workers formed red guards to defend the occupations from attack and to patrol the working class areas. Wisely, the government made no attempt to evict the occupiers, despite frantic pleas from some of the factory owners.

Italy's most influential newspaper, *Il Corriere dela Serra* of Milan, reported:

> Yesterday evening the factories presented a singular spectacle. One reached them through crowds of women and children, coming and going with dinners for the strikers. Entrances were strictly guarded by groups of workers. There was not the ghost of an official or police officer in sight and the strikers were complete masters of the situation. Whoever passed, in car or cab, was subjected to control as if he were crossing the frontier. And control was exercised by squads of workers.

One of the most important developments was the action of the railway workers. They began switching freight cars to the factory sidings, providing fuel, food, raw materials and transport connections between the various factories under occupation—enabling workers to continue production. The railway workers refused to transport troops being mobilised to defeat the struggle.

Gramsci argued that the movement had to go further and take over the real centres of power—the means of communication, the banks, the armed forces and the state. He addressed mass meetings and argued that workplace control and soviet democracy could only be achieved by making a revolution against the existing state. His emphasis on building factory councils came from his conviction that only with new, non-parliamentary institutions could the working class transform society.

His influence in Turin was decisive. But elsewhere the factory councils were under the control of the Socialist Party and the union officials. They saw the occupations as a tool for forcing the government to mediate with the employers and return things to normal.

The employers wanted troops sent in to clear the factories but prime minister Giolitti, not willing to attack the occupations for fear of raising the stakes, refused. In his 1975 book, *The Occupation of the Factories*, Paolo Spriano recounts a crucial conversation between Giolitti and Agnelli, the owner of Fiat:

> *Giolitti:* Only time can solve the problem. Otherwise there is no policy but force.
> *Agnelli:* Precisely.
> *Giolitti:* Maybe, but let us understand each other. I will not allow the security forces to stay in the streets, defenceless, if the red guards open fire from above. To drive the workers out of the factories we need artillery.
> *Agnelli:* I agree.
> *Giolitti:* We are in a position to supply it immediately. At Turin there is the 7th regiment of mountain artillery. I will give the orders at once. At dawn tomorrow Fiat will be bombarded and liberated from the occupiers.
> *Agnelli:* No! No!
> *Giolitti:* Well then?
> *Agnelli:* [No reply]

Giolitti later told the chief administrator of Milan:

> It is necessary to make the industrialists understand that no Italian government will resort to force and provoke a revolution simply to save them some money. The use of force will, at the vey least, ruin the factories. I place my faith in a peaceful solution.

Shrewdly, the prime minister relied on the trade union and Socialist Party leaders' desire for compromise. This enraged the employers but it opened the way for the PSI and the CGL to end the dispute.

With the establishment in a panic, the Socialist Party and CGL leaders met in Milan on 10 September. First the union leaders asked their Turin delegates if they were ready to lead an insurrection. Having been abandoned in April, Turin declined to stick their necks out again. The CGL then offered to hand the leadership of the movement over to the PSI if it wanted to fight for "political" rather than immediate economic demands.

For all their revolutionary bluster, the PSI leaders declined. Instead they demanded a referendum of the entire CGL membership on the question of revolution. Even their own supporters were puzzled: "A revolution is not made by asking a congress to decide whether there is going to be a revolution or not."

The deciding congress was not made up of delegates from the factory councils, but from the union branches—a deliberate move to exclude the most militant workers. Delegates representing 591,245 union members voted against revolution while delegates representing 409,569 members voted for. Given the lack of leadership and the exclusion of some of the most militant sections from the congress, it was an impressive minority vote for revolution.

Saving face

Angelo Tasca, one of the Turin leaders, was remorseless in his criticism of the PSI:

> The party directorate wasted months preaching the revolution. It had foreseen nothing, prepared nothing. When the vote in Milan gave a majority to the CGL theses, the party leaders heaved a sigh of relief. Liberated from all responsibility they could complain at the top of their voices about the CGL's betrayal. Thus they had something to offer the masses that they abandoned at the decisive moment, happy with an ending that allowed them to save their faces.

On 19 September, prime minister Giolitti summoned together the bosses and the union leaders and forced through a settlement giving a general wage increase and a promise to give the unions some say on how the factories would be run. The metal workers were balloted on the settlement by their leaders the following week.

With no alternative on offer they accepted by three to one. By the end of September all the factories had been handed back. A great revolutionary moment had been missed. Some of the leaders called it a victory, but hundreds of thousands who believed revolution was on the agenda returned to work demoralised.

On the bosses' side there was profound relief. Agnelli was so terrified he had offered to turn his company into a workers' co-operative. But the bosses' fear passed with rising unemployment and workers in retreat. Livid with the liberal Giolitti, the bosses would turn to the fascists to wreak revenge on the class that had so humiliated them.

In the introduction to his wonderful book on the factory occupations Paolo Spriano captures the mood at the height of the struggle:

> In the *Socialist Almanac* for 1921 there are some rare photographs of what the diligent compiler called "the most striking episode in the struggle being fought in Italy between capital and labour": the occupation of the factories in September 1920... What happened was an exceptional event and these images give us an immediate perception of it. Like Lenin far off, these hundreds of thousands of workers, with arms or without, who worked and slept and kept watch in the factories, thought the extraordinary days they were living through "the revolution in action".

For a month the workers had taken over the factories and run them without any pay. It was an incredible achievement. The occupations were spreading until the union leaders brought them to a halt. If the factory council movement could have broken out beyond Turin, the outcome could have been so different.

But the militants who wanted to extend the struggle and carry it towards an insurrection had no contact with each other and no contact with the peasants, ex-soldiers and landless labourers fighting in the south. By the time Gramsci had grasped the need to break with the reformist leadership of the PSI and launch the new Italian Communist Party, the occupations were over.

Looking back in 1924 Gramsci wrote:

> During 1919-20 we committed very serious errors, which we are now paying for in full. For fear of being called careerists, we did not form a separate fraction and try to organise it throughout Italy. We did not make the Turin factory councils into an independent directive centre, which could have exercised an immense influence over the whole country, for fear of splitting the trade unions and of being prematurely expelled from the Socialist Party.

Postscript: Italy 1945

The industrialists who bankrolled Mussolini to power in 1922 were happy with his regime until the Italian army suffered a series of defeats in 1943. The first mass resistance began in the spring of that year with a wave of strikes involving over 100,000 workers. Starting in Turin the strikes spread across northern Italy. Communist militants with memories of the Biennio Rosso were at the forefront. Mussolini told his followers that the strikes had set his movement back 20 years.

By the time Allied troops had landed in Sicily, the Italian ruling class was ready to ditch Mussolini to cling on to power. When they replaced him with Marshall Badoglio in July 1943, people flooded onto the streets of Rome to celebrate the end of fascism. But the celebrations were premature. The Nazis rescued Mussolini and the German army invaded northern Italy, installing a puppet government in Florence. This provoked a mass resistance movement, not least in the factories.

One of the enduring myths of the Second World War is that the Allies liberated occupied Europe. In Italy the partisans pinned down six of the 25 German divisions in northern Italy. They also liberated Naples, Florence and Milan. 700,000 Italians were involved in the resistance and for the first time in Italian history women came out of their homes in large numbers and got involved in politics.

There was a mass strike in Genoa in January 1944 after the Gestapo shot resistance fighters who had been taken prisoner. It was followed by a strike of 300,000 in Milan, which spread to Bologna and Florence, with low-paid women workers taking the lead. The resistance seized most of Florence from the Germans and took control of the factories before the invading Allied armies reached them. In Turin the brunt of the fighting fell on factory workers.

At the end of April 1945 workers seized control of Turin and Milan, and workers' councils were set up to run the factories. There was certainly plenty of evidence of the potential for workers' power. But it was not the workers who decided Italy's future; it was the leaders of the victorious superpowers—Roosevelt, Stalin and Churchill. They divided Europe into spheres of influence that suited each other's interests.

Stalin was not going to let Communists seize factories and lead revolutions in the West, for fear of the impact this would have on his rule in Eastern Europe. In 1944 the Italian Communist leader Togliatti returned from Moscow to announce that his party was joining the despised Badoglio government and would leave the monarchy in place until the war was over.

Factory on strike in Paris, June 1936.
(Photograph by David Seymour "Chim")

5·

FRANCE 1936: RED HOT JUNE

"The French revolution has begun".
—**Leon Trotsky, 9 June 1936**

WHAT STARTED as a factory sit-in to defend two sacked militants had, within a week, turned into a tidal wave of factory occupations that reduced the French bosses and their state to an absolute shambles.

The background to June 1936 was the world recession and the rise of fascism. Between 1931 and 1935 French output fell by a third. The economy was paralysed and workers suffered mass unemployment, factory closures and a fall in real wages. France was riven with political instability and government scandal.

In 1934 the French fascists, inspired by Hitler's triumph a year before, believed their time had come. On 6 February fascist gangs attacked the Palais Bourbon, a parliamentary building in Paris. Fifteen people were killed and thousands injured in the battle that followed. The government was forced to resign and was replaced by a right wing coalition of national unity.

The fascists believed they were emulating Hitler's road to power. They had anticipated little in the way of resistance from a working class which had suffered ten years of defeat. Yet the workers' response was magnificent. The sudden danger of fascism changed everything.

The CGT trade union called a general strike on 12 February and the Socialist Party (SFIO) called for a demonstration in Paris on the same day. Initially the leadership of the French Communist Party (PCF) denounced this call and their newspaper, *L'Humanité*, fumed, "How can we have unity of action with people who abandon the class struggle to collaborate in the defence of the capitalist system, and who, in France as in Germany, prepare the ground for fascism?"

As late as 11 February *L'Humanité* kept up its sectarian onslaught on the joint CGT/SFIO mobilisation, denouncing them as "social fascists". But during the night of 11 February the PCF leadership could not hold this line among its rank and file militants, who were demanding a united front with the CGT and the Socialists.

At the last moment the PCF decided to support the mobilisation. Five million joined the general strike and on the day two huge columns of marchers met in central Paris—one was led by the Communists, while a bigger one marched behind the Socialist leader Leon Blum.

Spontaneously, amid constant chants of "Unity, Unity", the two marches met and joined together into a million-strong demonstration. For the first time in years Socialist and Communist workers marched side by side. There were another 350 similar demonstrations in towns and cities across France. Workers were determined not to repeat the mistakes of Germany and let a French Hitler come to power.

The 12 February demonstration laid the basis for the French popular front. Hitler's victory had forced Stalin and the leaders of the USSR to do a U-turn and seek a military alliance with the then still dominant powers of France and Britain. A combination of Stalin's new foreign policy and the pressure for unity from rank and file workers had forced the PCF to abandon its grotesque non-cooperation with social democracy.

But in shifting to the Popular Front the PCF merely traded one disastrous policy for another, moving from criminal sectarianism to an unabashed patriotism.

Although the party had initially opposed an alliance with the socialists and trade union leaders, it now argued to extend this pact to include the Radical Party. The theoretical justification for this "broad front" was that it would signify an alliance between the working class, as represented by the Socialists and Communists, and the middle class, as represented by the Radicals. The PCF insisted that only such a broad alliance could block the growth of fascism.

The PCF pioneered this approach, but the popular front strategy was quickly adopted and applied everywhere Stalinism had an influence. Subsequent events in Spain proved that, rather than combating fascism, the popular front only served to confuse and disarm the working class. As Duncan Hallas explained in *Trotsky's Marxism*:

> As an auxiliary to Stalin's diplomacy—for that is what it had become—the Communist International was now jerked hard to the right. Its 1935 congress called for "the United Peoples' Front in the struggle for peace and against war... In the present phase a number of capitalist states are also concerned to maintain peace. Hence the possibility of creating a broad front of the working class, of all working people and of entire nations against the danger of imperialist war."
>
> Among those "capitalist states concerned to maintain peace" were the victors of 1918—the imperialist French and British ruling classes. These were the objects of Stalin's new line. Such a "front" was necessarily a defence of the imperialist status quo. Reformist rhetoric had to be employed to conceal this fact and for a time in France it succeeded.

By July 1935 the PCF and the SFIO reached an agreement with the Radical Party, the backbone of French bourgeois democracy. The three parties formed the

"Front Populaire"—an electoral alliance designed to bring the left to parliamentary office.

But the electoral arithmetic meant the Popular Front relied on the votes of the Radical Party and securing those votes meant doing nothing to upset its middle class supporters. On PCF insistence nationalisation was excluded from the Popular Front programme.

The positive aspect of the French Popular Front was that it reflected and fed off workers' desire for unity and radical change, and responded to and encouraged a rising wave of class struggle. Its formation fostered workplace activity and paved the way for the great upheavals of June 1936. It would take these upheavals to fully expose the conflict between workers' aspirations and the real aims of the Popular Front strategy.

The Popular Front manifesto called for the defence of civil liberties; the disbanding of the fascist squads; trade union rights; a reduction in the working week without loss of pay; jobs for the young; a new social security system with pensions and unemployment benefit; and world peace. Identifying with these slogans, half a million marched with the parties of the Popular Front through Paris on Bastille Day.

In February 1936 a Popular Front type government was swept to power in neighbouring Spain—the signal for mass action by Spanish workers and peasants. That same month half a million marched through Paris on an anti-fascist demonstration. On May Day 120,000 engineering workers stopped work. People saw the prospect of better times ahead. The left was optimistic as the French elections drew near.

All their expectations were exceeded when the Popular Front was elected on a big swing to the left. The Socialists, with 142 seats, were the largest group in the Chamber of Deputies, and the Popular Front had a majority of over 100 seats. The PCF doubled its vote, winning 72 seats. The first Popular Front government was to have been led by the Radical Party leader, Deladier, but the huge swing to the left meant it was Socialist Leon Blum who headed the new government.

The election results came in on the evening of Sunday 3 May and provoked spontaneous demonstrations and victory marches throughout the country. As the scale of the victory sank in, working class France sensed fantastic possibilities.

It was a triumph for the Socialists and Communists whose unity had halted the fascists two years before. But Maurice Thorez, leader of the PCF, signalled where Stalinism was headed when he claimed victory in nationalist terms:

> We deprived our enemies of the things they had stolen from us and trampled underfoot. We took back the Marseillaise and the Tricolore.

Socialist prime minister Leon Blum could not take over from the outgoing government for another month and, as he waited in the wings, the different classes made their moves. The rich panicked and the volume of capital leaving the country steadily increased. Impatient for real change and inspired by events in Spain, the workers moved to take matters into their own hands.

It began with two separate strikes in the aircraft industry within days of the election. In both cases workers demanded the reinstatement of militants sacked for going on the May Day march during working hours.

New features characterised both disputes: first, although workers went on strike, they stayed inside the factory to retain control and to avoid being locked out at a time of mass unemployment; second, the occupations got moral and physical support from local people; third, the entire workforce took part; and lastly they won total victory in a few days. These victories laid a pattern for everything that followed but with one exception—both struggles were defensive and that was about to change.

1930s France didn't have the same tradition of revolutionary agitation as Italy in 1920. It had no factory council movement, no Gramsci and no proletarian newspaper like *L'Ordine Nuovo*. Moreover, the Russian Revolution that had so inspired the Italian working class had been isolated and broken in the 1920s. The PCF was a bureaucratic party, firmly in Stalin's grip.

Occupations spread

None of this stopped French workers from fighting back. They knew from their own experience that ordinary strikes had meant police violence on the picket line plus the threat of being sacked or starved back to work. From that perspective, occupations made good sense.

The real start of the movement was the occupation on 14 May of the giant Bloch aircraft plant on the outskirts of Paris. The workers wanted higher wages and better conditions. Bloch's bosses caved in and one by one the Paris engineering factories put in similar demands and prepared to strike. By that point the movement had gone over to the offensive.

The 24 May was the date for the traditional Paris demonstration in memory of the martyrs of the 1871 Commune. The turnout was astonishing—600,000 people marched through the centre of Paris. Now workers could sense their collective power.

At Hotchkiss, one of the key Paris engineering factories, workers set down a list of demands based on what the incoming government had promised them. They occupied demanding union recognition, a significant wage rise, paid holidays, the abolition of overtime, no recriminations and full pay for the period spent occupying the factory. They won everything.

Suddenly workers understood they could get what they had voted for without waiting on the new government. When 35,000 Renault workers occupied on 28 May, it was the signal for every other engineering plant in Paris to follow.

On 29 May *L'Humanité* reported 100,000 out on strike and most of them in occupation. Action spread outside engineering as building workers on the Paris International Exhibition site struck. On 1 June the occupations spread to the smaller factories across Paris.

Thereafter strikes spread quickly throughout the chemical industry, the oil refineries, textiles, transport, food, the coal mines, shipyards, printing and furniture. The movement spread to Lyon, Lille, Vierzon, Rouen, Brive, Nice, Toulouse and Marseille.

By 4 June newspaper distribution, restaurants and hotels, locksmiths, jewellers, the clothing trade, gas, construction and agriculture were on strike and under occupation. Workers who had never been unionised occupied their workplaces. As the strikes spread, more of the ordinary public became involved. Public sympathy increased as shop assistants came out and publicised their starvation wages.

Within 14 days the movement had developed into the greatest strike wave the world had ever seen. Alexander Werth described the extraordinary sight of the Paris suburbs during June 1936: "Building after building, small factories, even comparatively small workshops—all were flying red or red and tricolour flags with pickets in front of the gates."

On 4 June Blum finally formed his government. President Lebrun took him aside and begged him to broadcast an appeal to the strikers:

> Tell them parliament is about to meet and that as soon as the session begins you are going to ask for an immediate

> passage of the social laws without further delay... They will believe you and then perhaps the strike movement will come to a halt.

The next day Blum did the broadcast but the movement didn't stop.

Instead the occupations spread across France and into areas where unions barely existed. The Paris department stores were occupied and the cinema industry, from the studios to the usherettes, went on strike. They put on films and shows for striking workers. Jean Renoir made his wonderful film, *Le Crime de Monsieur Lange*, in which Parisian workers take over their workplace, chase out the owner and run the concern as a workers' co-op.

A Popular Front supporter, who belonged to the Radical Party, complained at a party meeting:

> The occupation of the factories, shops and farms was not in the programme of the Popular Front. It is not only illegal; it is something worse—a humiliation for the employer. The occupations must cease.

At the height of the struggle 2 million were on strike in 12,000 workplaces, three quarters of which were occupied. Workers were in control, and to regain ground the bosses had no option but to agree massive concessions.

The Matignon Agreement

On 8 June prime minister Blum brokered the first Matignon Agreement between the government, the union leaders and the employers. The bosses accepted it completely. The deal guaranteed union recognition; collective bargaining; wage rises between 7 percent and 12 percent, graded so the lowest paid got the most; a minimum wage; paid holidays; a 40-hour week; and all backed by legislation and a guarantee of no victimisation.

The mass movement had circumvented parliament and implemented the entire Popular Front Manifesto from the bottom up, within four days of Blum taking office. The workers had made fantastic gains but they wanted more, and the union leaders had big problems convincing them to end the occupations.

Meanwhile, the movement continued to spread. Far from restraining the upheaval, Matignon was encouraging traditionally unorganised workers to join it. The cafe waiters came out and the hotels closed. In the countryside thousands of agricultural workers were on strike and occupying the farms. Action spread to North Africa. Thousands of unemployed workers occupied claimants' offices and invaded town halls, demanding the establishment of an unemployed fund and increases in benefit.

Events were moving in a revolutionary direction. In Paris, on the initiative of the militant Hotchkiss plant, delegates from 33 occupied factories organised a joint action committee—an embryonic workers' council. So Matignon mark two was hastily organised on 10 June. The union leaders were under pressure from the workers to negotiate for the previously agreed wage increases to be in addition to those already won locally. The best organised factories in Paris pledged to continue the occupations until all the demands were fully met.

Up to this point the Communist Party had encouraged the strikes and occupations. Indeed many rank and file Communist Party militants had initiated and led them. But as the government began to talk tough, the party shifted. To continue the struggle was to move towards revolution. On 12 June the government seized all copies of the Trotskyist paper *Lutte Ouvrière*, because it was calling for workers' power.

The Communist Party means order

That day the Communist Party issued a statement by leader Maurice Thorez:

> Given the development of campaigns by the right it is better not to use this form of struggle; given the development of reactionary campaigns that sow trouble and uncertainty among the common people...we must know how to end a strike.

On 14 June *L'Humanité* declared, "The Communist Party means order." From then on the PCF leadership spearheaded the return to work. Their argument was as follows: taking power was out of the question; the conditions were not ripe and to continue would risk isolation from the peasantry and the middle classes; this would destroy the Popular Front and open the door to the Nazis.

Stalin wanted an alliance *with* France, not a revolution *in* France. So the PCF fought to end the strikes and occupations, sacrificing the working class movement for the interests of the Popular Front government and Moscow. It was a disastrous strategy and it sealed the fate of the left in both France and Spain.

The first major return to work followed an agreement in the Paris engineering sector. The employers made further major concessions, notably for the lower paid. The influence of the Communists on the shop floor ensured a near unanimous acceptance by the factory delegates. One by one other industries settled and returned to work. Although sporadic strikes and occupations continued to break out, the great movement was effectively over.

The Popular Front celebrated Bastille Day with a million-strong demonstration, but the fight had ended. The joy and enthusiasm of June were briefly recaptured as workers and their families rushed to the seaside or the country to enjoy the first paid summer holidays they had ever known.

The Popular Front itself did not survive long after the ending of the occupations. In May 1937 Leon Blum was replaced by a more right wing leader and in 1938 the Popular Front government fell. The right was back in power and determined to wipe out the gains that workers had made.

In November 1938 a right wing coalition led by the Radical Party rescinded the 40-hour week won in 1936. The CGT called a strike, insisting on no demonstrations and no shows of strength. With such half-hearted, passive leadership the strike was patchy and the CGT called it off. At Renault the defeated workers were forced to march out of the factory through a gauntlet of pro-fascist policemen banging iron bars and shouting, "One for Blum, one for Timbaud [the Communist leader of the engineers' union] and one for Jouhaux [leader of the CGT]."

Moderation and patriotism did the Communist Party no good. In 1939 the parliament voted to outlaw the party and expel its deputies. Nine months later parliament voted to give dictatorial powers to Marshal Pétain, who formed a government with French fascists and collaborated with German Nazis. The recent French film *Army of Crime* paints an accurate picture of the terrible consequences.

A festival of the oppressed

Jacques Danos and Marcel Gibelin accurately described June 1936 as "a gigantic festival of the oppressed, which had shaken French society to its very foundations".

They pointed to the tremendous advances made by the movement and argued it could and should have gone on to take power:

> The extent of the social advances made should not be underestimated. The French working class had never before in its history won such a series of reforms, some of which were to remain almost unassailable by reason of the circumstances in which they had been wrenched from the employers.
>
> It is impossible, however, not to wonder whether June 1936 was something more than an industrial struggle of particularly huge dimensions, and especially whether it might have had much greater, immediate consequences.
>
> We should not forget that June 1936 happened at a time when the world working class was in retreat. The French struggle seemed to be a rearguard action. But could it not have been the starting point for a counter-attack, the beginning of a new upsurge in the working class movement throughout the world?
>
> The strike wave created the conditions for a revolutionary crisis in France...if the workers' struggle had indeed achieved the destruction of the capitalist state, the course of history might have been decisively altered.

Two important things were missing. There was no organisation of workers' councils to connect the struggles and challenge the power of the state and big business. The mood of the workers would have ensured that a call for such bodies would have received an enthusiastic response. But no one made the call.

The embryo of such a body was present in the initiative taken by the Hotchkiss workers—a local strike committee with delegates from 33 factories. If the occupations had lasted longer, or if the workers' assemblies that met to consider the Matignon Agreement had been more confident and forceful in opposing the Communist Party line, then this initiative could have spread.

The other missing factor was revolutionary political organisation. In every great movement from below individual militants with political ideas play a key role in determining the outcome of the struggle. 1936 was indeed a great movement and there were many thousands of militants who wanted to push the mass strikes and occupations into a challenge against French capitalism. There were many more thousands moving in that direction.

However, the best militants badly lacked a political organisation which could link them together and train them to counter the influence of the union leaders and the leadership of the PCF, who were peddling caution, moderation and nationalism in order to halt the momentum of the struggle and restore "normality".

Unfortunately the Trotskyists, who understood and opposed the treachery of Popular Front politics, were too few in number and too isolated to make any real impact.

The sit-down strike at Fisher Body Number Three plant, Flint, Michigan January-February 1937.

6.

THE US 1934–38: LABOUR'S GIANT STEP

> The intensification of labour is greater here, machinery is developing more rapidly and the worker is an old man in this country when he is still regarded as being in the prime of life at home. The emigrant sacrifices his future for his present for the sake of a few dollars more.
> **—James Connolly**

> The weakness of American unions was not due to any "exceptionalism" on the part of American workers, but rather the "exceptionalism" of the American capitalist class... American employers have opposed trade unions with a vehemence unequalled in any other OECD country... The decision to fight for the union was a much bigger decision for American workers than for those in Britain, a decision that often required an uncommon degree of anger and resolve. Once that decision was made they fought all the harder.
> **—John Newsinger, "1934: The Year of the Fightback", *International Socialism* 122**

In 1934 American workers burst into action and reached a level of militancy not seen since the great struggles that rocked the US in the aftermath of the First World War. Between 1934 and 1937 American workers unleashed the biggest strike wave in history and the sit-down became their essential weapon in the fight to build union organisation.

A new found sense of confidence had fused with a deep well of bitterness to produce one of the most dramatic transformations in working class history. By 1937 union membership was over 7 million—5 million up on the 1933 figure.

After the great wave of struggle at the end of the First World War had been defeated, the bosses decided to smash trade unionism in the US. As Newsinger writes:

> Once the unions had been contained the employers prepared for what has been described as "a war of extermination against organised labour". An open shop drive was launched across the country to smash the unions once and for all... The career of union organiser Fannie Sellins provides a useful case study on the role of repression...she was shot down in cold blood by company guards while picketing the Alleghany Coal and Coke Company mine in western Pennsylvania. Her skull was crushed with a blow from a club while she lay dead or dying. A coroner's jury returned a verdict that her killing was "justifiable self-defence", and went on to condemn "anarchy and Bolshevism".

It is difficult to exaggerate the magnitude of the defeat for organised labour. Throughout the "roaring twenties" the great corporations were free to accelerate their attacks and speed up work with new mass production techniques and tighter methods of supervision. Non-union workers faced a 12-hour day, had no rights and could be fired at will. Charlie Chaplin exposed these conditions and their numbing effect on workers in his film *Modern Times*.

In 1929, before the great slump, American unions, under the banner of the American Federation of Labour (AFL), organised only 3 million workers. The AFL was comprised entirely of skilled craft workers because its leaders dismissed unskilled labour as "un-organisable".

The lowest paid, including most women, immigrants and black workers, were largely excluded. And it meant that the burgeoning sectors of American capitalism—rubber, steel and the auto industry—remained unorganised.

American capitalism was dealt a devastating blow with the crash of 1929, and industrial production fell by 46 percent. Three years later it was still declining. For workers the depression was a disaster. Unemployment rose from 1.5 million in 1929 to 17 million by the end of 1932, when one quarter of the workforce was unemployed and the same number was working part time.

By 1931 employers were cutting wages across the board and by 1933 some 87 percent of firms had lowered wage rates at least once and some had done so several times, giving an average reduction of 18 percent.

300,000 farm workers were forced to migrate west to the "promised land" of California as the banks collapsed and small farms were repossessed. Folk singer and union organiser Woody Guthrie expressed the poverty and the broken dreams in the bitter humour of his "dust bowl ballads":

> California is a garden of Eden –
> A paradise to live in and see,
> But believe it or not, you won't find it so hot,
> If you ain't got the do re mi.

Half a million people became hoboes, travelling the roads and riding the railway boxcars looking for work. But the leaders of the AFL were not interested in the fate of the poor and the downtrodden. In 1932 they even opposed federal unemployment benefit. Their complacent attitude was summed up by the motto above the portal of the AFL headquarters, "Tomorrow is Another Day". Little wonder trade union membership was falling by 7,000 a week.

There were hunger marches and unemployed protests, but they were often brutally attacked. The government and the employers felt able to grind the faces of the poor. In 1932 an unemployed workers' demonstration at River Rouge was machine-gunned and four protesters were murdered. A demonstration of unemployed war veterans in Washington was ridden down by US cavalry.

When the presidential election was held in November 1932 after three years of economic meltdown, the mood was one of anger and desperation. President Hoover's Republican administration was doomed. Democrat Franklin Roosevelt was elected on a popular landslide and took office in March 1933. Roosevelt was portrayed as a friend of the unions—a myth that persists today.

Roosevelt's New Deal and the National Recovery Act

Elected on the promise of a "New Deal", Roosevelt's measures were mild, given the extent of the crisis, and their success in stabilising capitalism was very limited. The New Deal, and in particular the National Recovery Act (NRA), generally gave in to employer demands and appeared to be more concerned with preventing strikes than with protecting workers' rights and living standards.

It was part of a plan to save American capitalism. Roosevelt described himself as "the best friend the profit system ever had". But the NRA had an unintended impact. It included a section giving workers the right to union representation, and this raised workers' expectations. They began to flock to the unions in the belief that Roosevelt and the NRA would protect them.

The pro-union measures were limited and stemmed from Roosevelt's need to get the moderate union leaders on board to guarantee the working class vote and contain the growing signs of discontent from below. Nevertheless, working class America grew in confidence during the

New Deal years, making good use of Roosevelt's limited pro-union laws to organise struggle.

It was far from easy. For over a decade the unions had been in retreat and ruling class repression was intense. Free enterprise meant the corporations owned the law, the local police, the local newspapers, the local radio stations and the company towns built around their plants. There were 230 private detective agencies engaged in spying on unions as well as providing armed guards and strikebreakers. There were a minimum of 40,000 undercover agents at work in US industry.

Nonetheless the NRA strengthened workers' resolve to unionise, shifting the centre of struggle away from the hunger and unemployed protests towards strikes, with the start of 1933 seeing the biggest strike wave since the early 1920s.

But the union officials were able to quench the fire. Roosevelt, sensing weakness, sent in the National Guard to smash the strikes. In the first six months of his New Deal 15 strikers were killed, 200 injured and hundreds arrested.

The Communist Party's industrial strategy

As anger and bitterness mounted, the left began to grow, especially the Communist Party (CP), which grew from 7,000 to 28,000 between 1930 and 1934. The US CP was contradictory: it attracted the most class conscious workers and led strikes, yet at the same time it was loyal to Stalin's Russia and followed every twist and turn of its foreign policy. In 1934 the leadership lurched from ultra-left sectarianism to outright patriotism.

Despite its distorted politics, party members would play a key role in preparing the groundwork and leading some of the major battles that lay ahead. US labour historian and former General Motors car worker Roger Keeran, in his *The Communist Party and the Auto*

Workers' Union, described how the party made a serious and successful drive during this period to train its members and deepen its roots in industry, particularly in the huge car plants:

> In 1931 the CP developed a policy of concentration to focus the party's activity on the most decisive industries... Mass unemployment had so decimated the party's shop nuclei that less than 1 percent of its 14,000 members worked in large factories and the strategy of concentration was designed to overcome this isolation.
>
> Cleveland Communists selected the Fisher Body plant and Detroit Communists selected the two most notorious auto plants—Ford and Briggs. The Communists in Michigan placed auto workers in charge of the party branches in Flint... In 1932 a slight upturn in production enabled them to rekindle their activity in these plants. As more Communists became active in the workshops, more papers appeared. By 1935 there were 14 auto shop papers and between May 1935 and January 1936 12 shop units in Michigan put out 22 different issues.
>
> The typical shop unit consisted of ten members in a department of 700 workers. It met once or twice a week... A CP auto worker from Detroit explained: "In our meetings we discussed what we did last week, the contacts we met, the experiences we had and the successes and mistakes we made. We would discuss how we approached other workers and our plan for the coming week." The unit made a list of all workers in the department, decided whom to ask to join and whom to ask to buy the *Daily Worker* and pamphlets.
>
> Besides recruiting party members the nuclei tried to set up shop committees or basic union structures and to involve workers in struggle around their immediate grievances. Even small units produced an astounding amount of agitation. In conjunction with local non auto worker members

the unit held a weekly meeting and distributed literature at the gates. The main obstacle to party work in the shops remained the company's espionage system.

The Briggs strikes of 1933 represented the most serious example of auto worker protest that occurred in the pre-union recognition era. These strikes showed that the objective conditions of the depression and the subjective activity of the Communists and other socialists were creating a mass mood for unionisation even before the New Deal legislation and the arrival of AFL organisers. The strikes also demonstrated that even in the depths of recession workers could win significant concessions. Other socialists criticised the Communists for involving the unemployed on picket lines and for raising issues of black and white unity. In spite of the prominent role played by the Communist Party only a few auto workers joined the party but the party as a whole recruited a greater number than at any time since 1920.

In the end the most significant aspect of the Briggs strike was not that the Communists failed to win permanent gains for themselves and their union but rather that the strikes occurred at all, that they were led by Communists and that they represented a step towards complete unionisation.

At the beginning of 1934 the tide began to turn as the American economy staged a brief recovery with a modest fall in unemployment. As the threat of sackings and blacklisting eased, workers felt more confident in their ability to fight and union recruitment increased.

Although the textile workers were defeated in 1934, three other key strikes—the teamsters in Minneapolis, Auto-lite car component workers in Toledo and dockers on the West Coast—all won stunning victories. Fought almost simultaneously in the spring and summer of 1934, these successful battles shifted the momentum in favour of workers and raised the reputation of left wing socialists.

Each of the strikes was unofficial and illegal and the AFL leaders were swept aside. What set them apart from the previous strikes was that they were each the product of long, patient work by socialists, who had prepared the ground and taken the lead.

The outcome showed that however well armed and well funded the bosses' side, and however spineless or corrupt the union leaders, militant working class action could win. The new confidence had fused with the bitterness to generate a level of working class solidarity and resistance unprecedented since 1919.

Teamster Rebellion

In Minneapolis a small group of Trotskyists had spent years organising a union among the truckers. At the beginning of 1934 they were able to lead a small strike of 70 coal depot workers to victory. Now they could begin to build.

Farrell Dobbs tells the story in his book *Teamster Rebellion*. As a handbook for socialist militants it is hard to beat. Dobbs was a young worker with no clear political ideas. His ambition was to become a judge and make the world a fairer place. But his world changed with the Great Depression. Unemployed with a young family, he found a job with the Minneapolis Coal Company.

Soon after he started, there were cuts in hours and lay-offs and he found himself embroiled in one of the greatest battles in working class history—a series of strikes from February to August 1934, which involved mass picketing, a women's auxiliary, martial law and two strikers killed.

In the course of the dispute workers' ideas changed. Dobbs himself became a socialist after the first strike—joining the local Communist League, home to some of the best working class militants. The members of the Communist League looked to Trotsky instead of the more powerful Stalinist Communist Party, and the

Minneapolis branch coached Dobbs in both politics and the strategy and tactics of class struggle.

It was this combination which allowed them to lead the struggle to victory, despite brutal state repression and the treachery of their own leaders. The teamster rebellion developed into a general strike affecting the whole city. It created a situation of dual power in Minneapolis, as workers organised food distribution, and formed their own militia and medical corps.

The struggle became internationally famous after thousands of strikers fought a pitched battle with the police, in scenes shown to cheering cinema crowds throughout the US.

Following the victory trade unionism spread throughout the city. Minneapolis was a turning point in the class struggle, showing how workers could bypass their conservative leaders and how important a core of socialist militants was to this process.

The Toledo Auto-lite strike

The picture in Toledo, Ohio, was much the same. Supporters of the far left American Workers Party had organised unemployment protests and directed their work around the Toledo auto workers. They had already built a small but crucial base there before the strike began.

When the members of the AFL local (union branch) at Auto-lite first took strike action to win union recognition in February 1934, they were ordered back to work by the national president of the AFL. Six weeks later 4,000 walked out on strike again. But this represented less than half the workforce, and to make matters worse the AFL leaders accepted a court ruling to limit the number of pickets to 25.

No one expected this strike to end in victory, but the American Workers Party built a local solidarity movement that united employed and unemployed in a common struggle. This was crucial, for with over a third of Toledo out of work the company had planned to assemble an army of strikebreakers from among the local unemployed.

Instead the unemployed proved key to winning the strike. Through the American Workers Party's influence on the local Unemployed League, the strikers were able to convince thousands of unemployed workers not to take their jobs but to help them win the strike:

> Unity of the jobless with strikers was a cardinal principle with the revolutionaries of the American Workers Party. True to their word they mobilised 1,000 unemployed before the Auto-lite gates on the first day; 4,000 the next day; and 6,000 on the third day. [Sidney Lens, *The Labor Wars*, 1973]

A few weeks into the strike the pickets were attacked by scabs and the National Guard. 10,000 pickets defied a court injunction and then bombarded scabs inside the plant with rocks, using giant catapults made from rubber tyre inner tubes. After a 15-hour battle the National Guard finally rescued the strikebreakers trapped inside. The troops opened fire on the strikers, killing two and injuring dozens.

But the workers did not back down. They fought the National Guard for six days, and finally on 31 May the company agreed to close the plant to strikebreakers and the troops were removed. The next day 40,000 workers and unemployed protested outside the County Courthouse against the arrests of 200 strikers. Nearly all the city's union locals pledged a general strike in sympathy. The company backed down on 4 June, granting union recognition and agreeing to rehire all the strikers.

The San Francisco general strike

In the San Francisco docks a group of workers around the CP had launched a rank and file paper, the *Waterfront Worker*, in 1932. From that small beginning and through their success in a series of small disputes, they were able to build an all-out dock strike on the West Coast in 1934.

Just as in Toledo and Minneapolis, the dockers defied their own union when they struck in May 1934. Within two days 14,000 dock workers were out from San Diego to Seattle demanding a closed shop, a 30-hour week to replace the 44 hours then in place and union control over hiring. They wanted to replace the crooked system whereby foremen could pick those they wanted to work each day; where bribes and pay-offs to supervisors were necessary to get hired.

Union members elected Communist Harry Bridges as chair of the strike committee. Within a week the teamsters' union refused to move cargo to or from the docks and 25,000 maritime workers up and down the coast struck in solidarity. Meanwhile, the AFL president denounced the strikers as "communists".

Two months into the strike the San Francisco business community ordered the cops to open the port. The city sent in its entire police force, which opened fire on the crowd, launching a day-long battle that became known as "Bloody Thursday". Four workers were killed and hundreds more wounded. The strike committee spread the strike to other unions and a general strike paralysed the city for a week.

The police, the National Guard and vigilante squads unleashed a wave of repression against the strikers and raided the headquarters of the CP and all other socialist groups. But despite the treachery of their national union leaders, the strikers won union recognition and a partial victory that was remarkable in the circumstances.

All three revolts were tremendous examples of workers' power. Previously unorganised groups showed great militancy and courage. They defied the courts, and when the cops and the vigilantes attacked the strikers, delegations brought out other groups in support. Victory in all three struggles was gained by new methods and in defiance of the union bosses.

Each was run by directly elected strike committees and, crucially, the leadership of all three struggles came from left wing socialists and revolutionaries. Without the socialist politics, the patient preparation and the audacious leadership, none of these struggles would have succeeded.

The rise of the CIO and the spread of sit-down strikes

Inspired by these victories trade union activists in the auto industry began to recruit widely and looked for a way of replacing the narrow conservative trade unionism of the AFL with a fighting union based on the industry as a whole. The lesson was not lost on the union leaders. The AFL leadership saw the successful strikes were undermining craft unionism and resisted the development.

But others, led by the miners' leader John L Lewis, split from the AFL to form the Congress of Industrial Organisations (CIO) with the aim of recruiting millions of mass production workers into industrial unions. Lewis was a left bureaucrat with a reputation for top-down leadership. He acted as he did not so much from radicalism but because he could see the new type of unionism was coming, and he wanted to lead it rather than see it captured by the Communists and Trotskyists. These new developments inspired workers in hundreds of places to copy the militant methods which had brought the victories of 1934. In 1935 GM workers at Toledo struck for union recognition. It was a rank and file revolt and once again Trotskyists and Communists played a prominent role. Its victory sparked the formation of the United Auto Workers union, which affiliated to the CIO.

By 1936 workers' confidence was already surging, especially in the rubber and auto industries, and a wave of sit-down strikes spread through the key centre of tyre production—the town of Akron, Ohio, in early 1936.

The Akron workers at the Goodyear, Firestone and Goodrich tyre plants pioneered the "sit down" strike to stop management breaking strikes in December 1935 and January 1936. Mass pickets surrounded the Goodyear plant to prevent the cops bringing in strikebreakers. 10,000 workers sat down and won a big victory. A number of the key rank and file leaders were CP members.

The Akron sit-downs began over wage and union recognition issues, but the Akron Goodyear workers also sat down after company thugs beat up a local union leader. The next night the same group of workers sat down again—this time to protest at a racist Ku Klux Klan cross burning in full view of their Akron plant. Neither the CIO leaders nor Roosevelt could dampen the Akron workers' defiance:

> In late February 1936 Roosevelt sent his own mediator to convince Goodyear workers to end a two-week, company-wide sit-down. 4,000 workers at a mass meeting responded to the mediator's suggestion of a return to work with the chant, "No, no, a thousand times no, I'd rather be dead than a scab!" [Sharon Smith, *Subterranean Fire: A History of Working Class Radicalism in the USA*]

Sit-downs: a response to repression

The sit-downs came in response to the brutal repression meted out by the employers and their hired thugs. The car manufacturers and their parts suppliers had developed a powerful apparatus to break strikes and picket lines with physical force, tear gas and guns. The sit-down soon proved to be the best practical form of industrial action for countering and neutering employer and state violence.

The tactic did not occur spontaneously or fall out of the sky. Communist workers at Akron were at the forefront when the sit-downs kicked off. Henry Kraus, a CP activist in the UAW there, tells how the positive experience of the French occupations of June 1936 had been a big influence on UAW militants:

> The whole idea of the sit-down was that you were too exposed over the usual strike—strikes were illegal, you couldn't strike in Michigan...besides that there is the question of violence. You strike, you have a picket line, they'll break it up for sure, one way or another, and arrest people. So when we saw the French having their successful 1936, we saw this was brilliant—something we had to use.

During the final weeks of the presidential election campaign in1936 the CIO suspended its organising drives to devote its full resources to Roosevelt's re-election. The union leaders had cast the Democratic Party as the lesser evil compared to a Republican administration. This didn't go down well with many of the rank and file militants. Rising confidence had inspired workers to look beyond Roosevelt and the Democrats for a new political party to represent working people.

At the AFL and various other CIO conventions in 1935 and 1936 resolutions in support of forming a labour party gained considerable support. At the 1936 United Auto Workers convention delegates voted down a resolution supporting Roosevelt for president.

However, that did not stop the CIO leaders from ensuring the union's support for Roosevelt's re-election. That was one issue on which the AFL and CIO rivals agreed, and the CIO's loyalty to the New Deal coalition effectively prevented the launch of a labour party in the key election of 1936.

In 1935 Stalin had unveiled his new foreign policy of seeking allies among other world powers, including Roosevelt in the US. So after spending the previous seven years denouncing Roosevelt, the Democrats and reformists as social fascists, American Communists were instructed to work with them. As the 1936 election approached, Communists became uninvited supporters of Roosevelt's coalition and Communist shopfloor leaders were instructed to help the CIO leaders deliver working class votes for Roosevelt.

So at the very time workers were becoming radicalised on a large scale by the CIO strike wave, creating the potential for a revolutionary party, the Communist Party was working to block that potential. Despite the fact that many militants were ready to break with the Democrats, Roosevelt was re-elected on one of the biggest landslides in US history.

But this did not halt the radicalisation. Between 1936 and the end of 1937 the auto workers at the forefront of the CIO organising drives went on the offensive with the Flint sit-down strike in the winter of 1936-37 and the wave of struggle which washed across the US in the months that followed.

Flint: the great sit-down

There were 48 sit-down strikes in 1936, involving half a million workers. The biggest, most important and most famous began in December at General Motors in Flint, Michigan—the centre of GM's manufacturing empire, where the company had 15 plants.

Strikes had been tried at Flint in 1930 and again in 1934 but had been viciously broken by company stooges and the Flint police force.

GM was determined its workers would never join a union. Organisers and activists were targeted and driven out. Some were beaten up or "had accidents happen to them"; some were murdered. The company contracted the Pinkerton Agency to carry out surveillance. Hundreds of their spies worked in the plant, ever on the lookout for any worker thinking about joining the union. In 1934 alone GM spent $840,000 on "detective work".

It is claimed that GM used a fascist group called "The Black Legion", which tarred, feathered and murdered active trade unionists. GM treated workers like shit. "We hire Chevrolet workers from the neck down", boasted Arnold Lenz, Flint's Chevrolet plant manager in 1936.

The feeling among the union leaders was that General Motors could not be organised—the workers were too backward, the company too strong and brutal.

Of the 146,000 residents in Flint, 44,000 worked for General Motors. The company ran the city, controlling the main newspaper, the radio stations and the police force. Every city official—including the mayor, the chief of police and the judges—were either in the pay of GM or held stock in the company.

Genora Dollinger, a socialist whose husband Kermit Johnson was a union activist at the plant, and who later became known as "the Joan of Arc of Labour" for her role in the sit-down, described working and living conditions in Flint [quotes taken from S Rosenthal, "Genora Dollinger Remembers the 1936-37 GM Sit-Down Strike"]:

> We had a large influx come into the city from the deep south. They came north to find jobs with their furniture strapped on old jalopies. They'd move into a little one- or two-roomed hovel with no plumbing and no heating. Flint

was a GM town—lock, stock and barrel. These folks were so desperate they'd come and sit every day on the big lawns at the front of the plant in the hopes that a foreman would call them in to work for maybe an hour, a day or maybe a permanent job. That's how poor these workers really were.

Conditions were terrible inside the plants. You saw the Charlie Chaplin movie, *Modern Times*? Well that's exactly it. They'd men with stop watches timing the workers to see if they could squeeze more out of them. When "mother nature" called you had to wait for the foreman to summon a relief man to take your place on the assembly line... Management hired lip readers to watch men talk to each other to see if they were talking union. The first guy that ever wore a UAW button badge in the Chevrolet plant was fired immediately. They used to say, "Once you pass the gates of GM forget about the United States constitution." GM workers had no rights.

UAW recruitment

Yet in the summer of 1936 the infant UAW sent its organisers to Flint, knowing that if the plants there could be won for the union, the CIO and the UAW would have a bridgehead into American industry. The key union organiser was Wyndham Mortimer, who had led a UAW strike in Cleveland and was a member of the Communist Party.

The union knew GM only had two factories that produced the dies from which the body components for all their many other factories were stamped. One was at Fisher Body Number One plant in Flint, the other at the Cleveland Body plant. The union strategy was to recruit enough members to be able to call a strike in both plants early in 1937.

The novel recruitment drive met with immediate success, and the union gained a foothold in the Flint plants.

Virtually every Flint household had at least one member working in an auto plant. Instead of speaking in meeting halls, the union organisers went door to door, signing up new members and keeping those names secret from others in Flint and from the UAW headquarters. This allowed the union to keep its new membership lists out of the hands of the many company spies who posed as union members.

But as Dollinger explains, it was anything but easy:

> The daily newspaper, the *Flint Journal*, was controlled completely by GM. They wrote things like, "You don't bite the hand that feeds you—these people coming in here are all imports from Soviet Russia and they want communism." The radio stations were controlled by GM too. The only thing the union had at first was mimeographed sheets. Finally we were able to put out a weekly Flint *Auto Worker*—with reports of what the union was doing, what we were working for, what kind of society we wanted. We handed these out at the plant gates after work. The distributors often got beaten up by the company's agents. They had Pinkerton spies there plus GM protection police. It was a dangerous period—no question about it.

The work of socialists and communists, both inside and outside the plant, was crucial in the immediate recruitment drive and in preparing and shaping the confrontations that lay ahead:

> Fermentation was taking place for a couple of years before the first sit-down. No question about it. Many so-called revolutionaries talk about "spontaneous combustion of workers". I can't see that at all because it took time and hard work for the organisers in various plants of the whole GM empire to talk to the workers, make contact, bring them to classes, create a bond.

A considerable amount of preparatory work was done before the strike by socialists. We had several very active organisations in Flint and Detroit: the Communist Party, the Socialist Labour Party, the Socialist Party and the IWW. Two years before the strike the Socialist Party in Flint held meetings in garages and basements—secret meetings so people wouldn't get caught and beaten up. These talks helped produce leaders for the coming struggle.

I was keen on building the Socialist Party. As we got bigger the party sent us their speakers from New York. We put out leaflets and sold tickets for these meetings, which were held in the basement of the Methodist Church. We held lectures in socialism plus labour history and current events—focusing on what was happening politically. Those were very popular meetings and we would get 300 or 400 at them.

This was all before the strike—in preparation for when the struggle actually broke out. A core of socialists understood that this would eventually happen. Our Socialist Party was the next biggest organisation to the Communist Party. Our newspaper, the *Socialist Call*, was distributed widely to help recruit GM workers into the party. We laid a solid groundwork, for some of the first people to act were Socialist Party workers.

The Communist Party met at the north end of Flint because that's where most of the immigrants from Russia, Poland and Hungary lived. They had a lot of social activities and political meetings. Robert Travis, the top UAW organiser in Flint, was in the Communist Party and selected Roy Reuther, a Socialist Party member, as his second in charge during the strike.

GM climb-down

Stickers began to appear on auto bodies, carrying the union message down the assembly line. Confidence was growing and in November 1936 the union won a series of small sit-downs in Fisher Body Number One, which boosted morale.

In one instance a foreman eliminated one man from a three-man team and told the other two to do the work. The two men, who were not in the union, stopped work. They were fired and thrown out of the plant.

Outrage spread throughout the plant, which employed 7,000, and soon it was at a standstill as workers sat down. A committee was elected to meet with the superintendent. Nothing like this had ever happened at any of the body plants before. The company agreed to rehire the two workers who had been fired and not dock the other employees for the time lost in the stoppage. That wasn't enough. The strikers demanded the two employees be brought back to the plant immediately.

General Motors had to broadcast over local and police radio to find the two men, one of whom was on a date with his girlfriend. Work didn't resume until he had driven her home, changed his clothes and taken his place on the assembly line. After that workers flocked to the union.

The union's aim had been to move immediately in the new year—but it had to accelerate its original plan, when the Cleveland Body plant went on strike on 30 December. The UAW immediately announced it would not settle the Cleveland strike until it reached a national agreement with GM covering all of its plants.

The same day the union discovered that GM was planning to move the dies out of Fisher Body Number One, so the Flint sit-down strike began there and then. It would last 44 days and change the history of American trade unionism.

Inside the plant the workers moved unfinished car bodies in front of all the entrances, forming a barricade. They welded a steel frame around every door and placed bullet-proof metal sheets over every window, drilling threaded holes into them so the nozzles of fire hoses could be screwed into them. They soaked clothes and kept them in readiness to cover their faces in the event of a tear gas attack. Large supplies of metal parts were placed at strategic points and paint guns for spraying would-be invaders were located throughout the plant.

The workers in Fisher Number Two sat down within minutes of the takeover of Fisher Number One. The production of GM auto bodies came to a standstill and on 1 January 1937 all Chevrolet and Buick assembly plants were closed.

Democracy at work

Mass meetings elected a series of committees to run the sit-in—strategy, food, security, information, sanitation, entertainment and education. Changes in the composition could be made at any of the twice daily meetings.

The security committee guarded every plant entrance and posted the name and shift of every one on the bulletin boards. It organised a complete walk round of the plant every hour, 24 hours a day, throughout the entire strike.

Every worker in the plant had a specific duty for six hours a day. A plant post office was established to handle all mail. Daily visits were arranged and workers' children could be handed through a window while workers talked to their wives as they stood outside.

There was a sit-in orchestra composed of strikers and concerts were broadcast over the plant's loudspeaker system every evening. Detroit's Contemporary Theatre put on plays. Charlie Chaplin donated his then current movie, *Modern Times*, and showings were held inside the plant. Students led writing classes and workers tried their hand at writing plays.

Outside the plant the union set up committees for food preparation, publicity, hardship, picketing and union recruitment. The responsibility of feeding several thousand workers both inside and outside the plants every day was enormous. Transportation of the food was provided by the city's bus drivers—the auto workers had supported them during a recent strike of their own.

Several hundred workers loaned their cars to the union and they toured Flint with loudspeakers. A special newspaper was produced and the union picketed the plant round the clock. The union set up a nursery to take care of the children while their mothers were working for the strike.

General Motors obtained an injunction ordering the workers to vacate the plants within 24 hours. But when the union's lawyers discovered that the judge owned over $200,000 worth of GM stock the injunction was quite literally laughed out of court.

As the occupation grew in strength General Motors upped the violence. The playwright Arthur Miller visited the Flint occupation as a young journalist and described the scene:

> Three National Guardsmen were tending a machine gun...they had fired on three workers taking the air on the roof, wounding one of them. Other soldiers moved around silently, rifles unslung, and a couple of army trucks filled with young troopers blocked both ends of the street. Two overturned police cars lay at odd angles, upended by a powerful stream of water from fire hoses manned by workers, who had connected them to hot water outlets to keep police and soldiers at bay.
>
> To prevent invasion through the covered overpass, they had welded it shut with several Chevrolet bodies set vertically on end. This was the third day of the strike. There

was a silence broken only by a muffled saxophone from inside the plant, where an improvised jazz group would periodically blow up a few numbers.

On 11 January the women delivering the evening meal to the strikers occupying Fisher Body Number Two found the plant surrounded by company guards, who were blocking the door normally used for the food delivery. The women started passing food in through windows. The guards fired tear gas into the plant and into the group of women.

As news spread, hundreds of workers raced to the scene. Some were union members from Buick and Chevrolet; some were "flying squads" from Toledo. The outside picketers from Fisher Body Number Two fought with the company guards, using homemade clubs. They succeeded in taking the guards' keys and regained control of the plant perimeter.

Members of the Flint police department arrived to reinforce the company guards. Again tear gas was fired into the plant and into the crowd of union sympathisers. Workers occupying the plant retaliated with water from the high-pressure water hoses and by pelting the police with milk bottles, stones and steel auto hinges, which they threw from the roof of the plant.

When the wind changed direction the tear gas that had been fired into the crowd outside the plant blew back into the ranks of the police and they retreated. After regrouping, the police returned in a second attempt to oust the workers; again they were met with a volley of hinges and milk bottles.

The police finally drew their pistols and opened fire, shooting into the crowd of union supporters at almost point-blank range. Fourteen workers were wounded but others overturned the sheriff's car, forcing the police to retreat.

Genora Dollinger, who had helped establish the women's auxiliary, took over the sound truck and drove round the town broadcasting:

> Cowards! Cowards! Shooting unarmed and defenceless men! Women of Flint! This is your fight! Join the picket line and defend your jobs, your husband's job and your children's home.

Soon a group of 400 women arrived, wearing bright red berets and armed with homemade clubs. This was the Women's Emergency Brigade, organised by the strikers' wives. They broke through the ranks of the police and made their way to the factory.

The police attacked again but, now outnumbered, they retreated and did not return. Casualties included 16 wounded strikers, mostly with bullet wounds, and 11 wounded police officers, who had been struck by thrown objects.

"Bull" was American slang for a cop. Their failed attempt to break the sit-down became known as "The Battle of Bulls Run". The strikers celebrated the outcome and thousands more joined the union.

The Women's Auxiliary

Women helped transform the sit-in. 23 year-old Genora Dollinger was a key organiser of the Women's Auxiliary and its military wing, the Women's Emergency Brigade. She recalls having to argue with some of the men:

> After the first sit-down started I went to the picket line to help. One of the leaders said, "Go to the kitchen, we need help there." They didn't know what else to tell a woman to do. I said, "You got a lot of skinny little men around here who can't stand to be out on cold picket lines for very long—they can peel potatoes as well as any woman."

Instead I organised a kids' picket. We could only do that once because it was too dangerous but we got a lot of good publicity. The picture of my two year old holding a picket sign saying "My Daddy Strikes for us Little Tykes" went all over the world and people from France sent me newspaper articles about it. It was remarkable that news of our strike travelled so far.

After that we organised the Women's Auxiliary. We held speaking classes for the women—most of whom had never been to a union meeting. Some men said the women who came down the picket line were only looking for men. But as more married men with families became active in the strike and saw what we could do, they kept those elements quiet. We won respect and organising women in the strike was the most wonderful experience of my whole life.

After the "Battle of Bulls Run", Roosevelt pressured GM into meeting the UAW on 13 January to agree a deal, and it looked like the workers had won. As they prepared to march out of the occupations with banners flying and bands playing, news leaked out that the company was negotiating with the scab Flint Alliance and would not concede sole negotiating rights to the UAW. The barricades went up again and the sit-ins continued.

GM snatched the initiative. Plants they had shut at the beginning of the strike were reopened. By now it was clear that the union would have to halt all GM production. Across the road from the Fisher Body plants stood the Chevrolet factories. Most notable among them was Chevrolet Number Four, GM's biggest plant and the sole source of all Chevrolet engines. The problem for the UAW was that 1,500 armed guards patrolled this plant and its assembly lines were riddled with company spies.

General Motors were confident that Chevrolet Number Four, which employed 7,000 workers, was impregnable. They upped the stakes by obtaining a second court injunction against the other sit-ins. The UAW not only ignored this order, but decided to take over Chevrolet Number Four.

On 29 January organiser Bill Travis called a meeting of Chevrolet union members. At the end of it 30 "trusted" members were selected and asked to stay behind. They were given instructions as to how the union would respond the following day.

The 30 included some men known to the union as company spies, and they were told that at exactly 3.20 on Monday 1 February the union would take over Plant Nine, which had the strongest union presence and would be the easiest for sit-down strikers to defend

Only six key UAW activists—Kermit Johnson being one of them—knew that this was a ruse and that the real target was the heavily guarded Plant Four.

The union issued a call for a protest march on 1 February. As a huge crowd assembled for the march, a member of the Women's Emergency Brigade rushed up to one of the organisers and handed him a slip of paper. He unfolded the paper and told the crowd, "They're beating up our boys at Chevy Nine. Let's get down there." The slip of paper was, in fact, blank.

Since the company knew that the first action was to take place at Plant Nine, its entire police force had been stationed nearby. When, at 3.20, workers marched into the plant yelling "Strike!" the company police stormed in and began beating the workers.

At 3.45, while the battle at Plant Nine was raging, the manager at Plant Four raced through the assembly lines, ordering all of the company spies and security men over to Plant Nine to reinforce the guards and security personnel there.

Plant Four was now devoid of guards, security personnel and company spies. At 4.10 union leaders inside

Plant Nine acknowledged "defeat" and got the union members to leave the plant.

But in Plant Four the union members led by Kermit Johnson stopped the machines and evicted the foremen from the plant. Plant guards returning from their "victory" at Plant Nine tried to re-enter Plant Four, but were driven off by strikers armed with pistons, connecting rods and rocker arms. Hundreds of women came down the hill towards Plant Four. They assembled in front of the gates and locked their arms together.

The women were first in line if there was any attempt to re-take the plant. The union had achieved the impossible by capturing Chevrolet Number Four. But could they hold it?

The next day GM turned off the heat in Number Four so the workers threatened to light bonfires to keep warm. GM restored the heating. On 8 February the company secured a second injunction to evict the occupiers and mobilised the National Guard, 1,000 armed vigilantes and the Flint police.

Inside the occupied factories workers voted to hold the plants at all costs and prepared for a siege. "That morning", wrote Art Preis, "all roads into Flint were jammed with unionists from Detroit, Lansing, Pontiac and Toledo." Outside, 20,000 GM workers and supporters surrounded Fisher Body Two, while the solidarity contingent, including over 1,000 veterans from the Toledo Auto-lite strike, rubber workers from Akron and coalminers from Pittsburgh, formed a ring around Fisher Body One, ready to do battle.

Meanwhile Flint city officials began arming anti-union vigilantes and the chief of police stated:

> Unless John L Lewis wants a massacre, he had better call off his union men. The good citizens of Flint are getting out

of hand. We are organising fast and will have 1,000 men ready for any emergency.

Lewis responded:

> I do not doubt your ability to call out your soldiers to shoot the members of our union out of those plants but let me say that when you issue that order, I shall leave this conference and I shall enter one of those plants with my own people. And the militia will have the pleasure of shooting me out of the plants with them. [Quoted in S Smith]

Victory is ours

Finally, on 11 February, the 44th day of the sit-in, with tens of thousands of workers ready to fight and threatening to wreck the factories, General Motors surrendered. Some 140,000 of their 150,000 workforce were sitting in or picketing. America's biggest company was forced to recognise the United Auto Workers.

Under a banner proclaiming "Victory is Ours" the sit-down strikers marched out of the plant singing "Solidarity Forever":

> Thousands of wives, children and well-wishers showered them with balloons, confetti and flowers. The throng marched to the Fisher Number Two and Chevrolet Number Four, where repeated scenes of jubilation occurred. After a procession through downtown Flint the strikers and their supporters gathered at the Pengally Hall for a victory rally and songs. Never had anything like this been seen in Flint. [S Smith]

It was an enormous victory for the working class, the first time in the history of the United States that any employer had granted exclusive bargaining rights to any union on a national basis.

In 1937 there were 477 sit-down strikes involving every kind of industry and trade—Chrysler workers, Woolworth shop workers, Western Union messengers, restaurant and hotel employees, refuse collectors, print workers, glass blowers and tyre builders. Soon sit-down strikers everywhere were singing the lyrics of the "Sit-Down" song:

> When they tie the can to a union man, Sit down! Sit down! When they give him the sack, they'll take him back, Sit down! Sit down! When the speed-up comes, just twiddle your thumbs, Sit down! Sit down! When the boss won't talk, don't take a walk, Sit down, Sit down!

The sit-down tactic became universally popular as a form of protest, as Art Preis notes:

> People sat down at relief offices, in employment agencies and against the police at eviction demonstrations. Prisoners adopted the tactic in the jails of Joliet, Illinois and Philadelphia. Children did the same in movie theatres to protest at programme cuts.

On 2 March, US Steel, the largest steel company in the world, signed a contract with the CIO-sponsored union without a strike. Within a year membership of the UAW grew from 30,000 to 500,000 and wages for car workers increased by as much as 300 percent.

There was a spiritual growth too, as the strikes and sit-ins brought a new sense of power and made workers more political. Union membership among women trebled and the CIO actively recruited black workers. As Chris Harman wrote in *A People's History of the World*:

> The strikes had the potential to change the whole culture of US capitalism by challenging the pervading individualism—

the myth of the American dream that everybody could get ahead—and the racism that was the other side of this. Where the unions were successful they began to create a new culture of collective action among American workers—summed up by the union song, "Solidarity Forever", sung in the sit-ins—and began to chip away at the racism in cities like Detroit. The CIO was the only large-scale institution in US society where blacks had a chance of genuine participation alongside whites.

Alas, the potential of the movement was never fulfilled because the politics which dominated the left stopped it from going forward.

The role of the Communist Party

The CP was not the only socialist organisation fighting to lead the movement. The 1934 strikes in particular had shown that Trotsky's supporters were both talented and capable and had better general politics. But they were far too few in number. The CP was the only genuinely national force on the left capable of giving a decisive lead. At the start of the depression the CP claimed 7,500 members compared with the 130 or so Trotskyists.

By the end of 1938 the CP had grown to over 80,000 while the Trotskyist Socialist Workers Party had around 3,000 members. More importantly, the CP built a powerful base among industrial workers, including many of the shopfloor leaders who'd built the CIO unions in struggle. In these conditions the Communists greatly increased their membership and standing in the movement.

In 1935 they had 630 auto workers and by 1938 the figure was over 1,100, with a very much larger periphery of sympathisers. In 1937 the CP had 28 factory units in the Detroit car plants and CP members were active in nearly every major auto workers' union local.

Rank and file CP members led some of the key rubber workers' strikes that engulfed Akron in 1936, and there is absolutely no doubt that party members played a decisive role both in the preparation of the Flint campaign and throughout its 44 day duration. Roger Keeran explains:

> The major fact to keep in mind is that the whole strategy of the sit-down was Communist inspired, Communist directed and Communist controlled. Though the strike certainly did not arise from a Communist plot, the Communists supplied a core of experienced and selfless people who participated in every aspect of activity. The Communists also had much to do with the entire strategy of the sit-down, from preparation and timing of the original work stoppage to the capture of Chevrolet Number Four and the decision to hold the plants by force, if necessary. Years later Wyndham Mortimer said that while many non-Communists played prominent roles, "the main strategy of the sit-down strike itself was conducted by the Communists. I think the Communists had a lot to do with winning the strike." No person involved in that momentous affair was in a better position to know.

The CP's leading role in the Flint struggle was borne out by local recruitment:

> The sit-down strikes produced immeasurable political and organisational benefits for the Communist Party...they brought socialist consciousness to more auto workers than did any other radicals of previous years in any mass production industry... The Communists expanded their influence among Detroit's ethnic working class. The social clubs and halls of Polish, Russian, Slovakian, Ukrainian, Finnish, Lithuanian, Hungarian, Armenian and a dozen other ethnic groups became centres of Communist social and political life.

In the 1930s the CP still claimed to be the inheritors of the tradition of the 1917 Revolution. Stalin's atrocities were hidden outside of Russia until the 1950s. In the face of triumphant fascism in Italy, Germany and Spain, the Russian Revolution still provided inspiration to workers struggling against the recession, and Stalin could pose as a bulwark against fascism.

This gave the CP an undoubted influence among class conscious workers during the period—making the consequences of its misguided policies all the more damaging for the US working class movement towards the end of the decade.

Supporting Roosevelt's New Deal coalition had a devastating effect on the class struggle as Communists gave the CIO officials their support and the CP used its influence inside the unions to lead workers away from militancy.

At the start of the Flint sit-down John L Lewis, leader of the CIO, was quick to issue a statement of support—not because he approved of the tactic but because he wanted to unionise the car industry under the CIO banner. But once Flint was over, Lewis fought hard to impose his will on the union militants, and the CP helped him to succeed.

Lewis insisted that the CIO would not tolerate unauthorised action and assured employers, "CIO contract is adequate protection against sit-downs, lie-downs or any other kind of strike." But his words were ignored by the militants and there were another 200 wildcat strikes and sit-downs in the four months after GM had signed their first agreement. In mid-1937 the UAW leadership issued a formal statement that the union would not allow strikes without formal union authorisation.

The trade union bureaucracy's political attachment to Roosevelt led it to dampen the strikes and outlaw sit-ins at Chrysler. Lewis could rely on the influence of the CP to hold workers back, although on occasions militants—including Communists—ignored Lewis and the CP leadership.

So the *Daily Worker* carried a statement from the leadership, which declared:

> Communists and the Communist Party had never in the past and do not now in any shape or form advocate or support unauthorised and wildcat actions... If party members were to initiate such action it would be gravely injurious to the cause of the cooperative action between labour and middle class groups.

The party was prepared to disavow unofficial strikes and sit-ins rather than break with Lewis. The grassroots militancy of 1934 to early 1937 gave way to tight control from above. At the very point where masses of workers were becoming politicised by the industrial struggle, creating the potential for a revolutionary workers' party, the CP did everything it could to abort this process.

Workers in steel went on strike but didn't occupy and the employers locked them out. The abandonment of radical tactics by the CIO leaders was responsible for the failure to break into the steel industry, halting the movement's forward momentum:

> It was to be expected that Roosevelt would turn his back on the labour movement and that the CIO leadership would not lead a fight against Roosevelt. But by the time workers learned this bitter lesson, the greatest upsurge in US history was over. [S Smith]

Lewis had defended the Communists for as long as they suited his purpose: "I do not turn my organisers or members upside down to see what kind of literature falls out of their pockets." But when he no longer needed the CP organisers he sacked them from the union's payroll.

If the best sections of the movement had broken with Roosevelt and the union leaders; if the sit-downs had been escalated instead of being curtailed in 1937, it would have created the conditions for building a revolutionary party rooted in the working class that was big enough to influence the course of the struggle.

The CP was large enough—not only had it increased its industrial base among workers, but by 1937 it had won leading posts in nearly half of the CIO unions. But it had ceased to be revolutionary; instead of leading workers forward it abandoned them. In the eyes of militant workers, the Communist Party blew it when it turned its back on the rising class struggle in 1937.

Nonetheless, the strikes and sit-downs of the 1930s remain the high point in US working class history and a source of inspiration for workers today. In a few short years American labour really did take a giant step.

7.

FRANCE 1968: DEMANDING THE IMPOSSIBLE

1968 WAS the year the world caught fire. The flames of revolt inspired a generation and shaped struggles around the world for a long time to come. 1968 is remembered as the year of student rebellion but it is conveniently overlooked that the student unrest was only the beginning of what would quickly become the biggest workers' general strike ever seen.

May was the most eventful month of a turbulent year. Parisian students, angered by the Vietnam War, clashed with the university authorities and the police. A series of struggles culminated in the "night of the barricades" on the evening of 10 May, when thousands of students fought pitched battles with the CRS riot cops and drove them from the Latin Quarter.

De Gaulle's authoritarian government had seemed invincible. Wages and employment policies were imposed without consultation by a government that ruled by decree. CRS riot police were regularly used to attack strikes and break workers' picket lines. By 1966 French industrial workers were the second worst paid in the European Common Market and working the longest hours. They also paid the highest taxes.

The same austerity dominated the universities. Student numbers were expanded in an attempt to meet the needs of modern French capitalism, but there was virtually nothing in the way of material provision to cope with the rapid increase of students. Compared to

The occupation at Renault Billancourt, Paris, May 1968.

Germany, Britain and the US, French universities were particularly bad when it came to overcrowding and underfunding.

In 1968 the Communist Party (PCF) was still by far the most significant organisation on the French left. For over 20 years it had commanded around 20 percent of the vote in nearly every election. It controlled the CGT and enjoyed a virtual monopoly in the industrial working class. But in the student movement its political rivals—including Maoists, Trotskyists and anarchists—were gaining ground. For the PCF leaders the rising student struggles were less important than the need to maintain their grip on the working class movement.

At first this was not a big problem for the PCF because the student protests seemed isolated. Party leader George Marchais denounced the first confrontations between the students and the police as:

> the work of ultra-leftists. For the most part they are the sons of the rich bourgeois...who will quickly turn off their revolutionary ardour and go back to managing Daddy's firm.

But attitudes towards the students changed as a result of the police violence. When the students proved that they were not only ready to fight the police, but were also able to stand their ground, thousands of young workers joined them, pouring into the Latin Quarter to take part in the demonstrations. One of the Young Communist leaders in Paris explained:

> I had difficulty in holding the lads back. One simple word from the party and they would have rushed to the Latin Quarter. That authorisation never came but some comrades went anyway and demonstrated in crash helmets.

The evening of 10 May was decisive. That night the battle between the students and the CRS riot cops was broadcast live to the nation by the local radio stations. The CRS had attacked the students with tear gas and truncheons. The students built barricades and defended themselves with cobblestones. Millions were shocked and angered by the police brutality and many were inspired by the students' courage.

For years the PCF had been trying to prove it was responsible and could do deals with social democratic politicians, hoping eventually to participate in a coalition government. The last thing it wanted to do was advocate direct action by students, but it could not ignore its rank and file base. The widespread sympathy for the students forced the PCF and the CGT to act.

In an effort to take credit and contain the protest, the union leaders called a one-day general strike and mass demonstrations against the police violence for Monday 13 May. It was meant to act as a safety valve, but it had the opposite effect. Ten million stopped work and over a million marched through Paris.

Hundreds of thousands of trade unionists with factory and union branch banners joined tens of thousands of university and high school students carrying the red and black flags from the "battle of the barricades" of two nights earlier. At the front of the demonstration was a great banner reading "Students, Teachers, Workers, Solidarity".

It was the largest demonstration the city had seen since its liberation from Nazi occupation in 1944. The huge numbers gave workers a sense of their own power. The demonstration dispersed peacefully and the government assumed it would mark the end of the student agitation. So did the trade union leaders. It could have been the end of the story but for the workers at the Sud Aviation aircraft factory in Nantes.

Nantes leads the way

Up to this point the Sud Aviation workforce had been holding a symbolic 15-minute strike every Tuesday to demand that short-time working imposed because of falling orders should not lead to a cut in their wages. That particular Tuesday, the day after the general strike, young workers in one section of the plant refused to return to work after the 15-minute protest was up.

Instead they marched through the factory gathering support. They rounded up the management, locked them up, and subjected them to continuous playing of the "Internationale", while 2,000 workers barricaded themselves inside the factory and began an occupation. The Sud Aviation plant was not a bastion of the trade union movement, but there were Trotskyists active in the section that initiated the protest.

The next day the Renault gearbox plant near Rouen occupied. It was a new factory with young workers from the countryside. They had no tradition of militancy. Only a minority of them had come out on Monday's general strike. When they learned that 10 million workers had taken strike action they felt ashamed. At midday on the Wednesday they heard about the events at Sud Aviation and decided to make amends with a copycat action. So they locked up the managers, barricaded the factory and occupied it.

Many more factories occupied, including the Lockheed plants at Beauvais and Orleans and the Renault plants at Flins and Le Mans. Later that evening the giant Renault Billancourt plant—the biggest and traditionally the most influential factory in Paris—was occupied. Over 80,000 workers were now involved and every radio and TV news bulletin reported more and more factories being occupied.

The Renault Billancourt occupation was decisive. The PCF attempted to stop the occupation but angry young workers under the leadership of militants from the Trotskyist Lutte Ouvrière and the Maoists forced the issue. The PCF decided it was better to put itself at the head of the occupation than to continue to oppose it.

Michel Certano had joined Renault as a 15 year old apprentice in 1958. By 1968 he was a young CGT union shop steward and took an active lead in the occupation. He explains the significance of what happened:

> We started the occupation at Renault Billancourt on Thursday 16 May. We held meetings every day where workers could vote on the continuation of the strike. We were occupying day and night and the movement was so exhilarating for us young people. 25,000 workers were on strike in our factory. Renault Billancourt had the biggest concentration of workers and it had a long history of struggle—that's the reason why the strike was so important. President de Gaulle had to rush back from a trip to Romania because we had occupied. Prime minister Pompidou said, "Now it's serious!" Everyone knew what Renault represented. It was the biggest factory in France.

The occupations led to a dramatic rise in class consciousness. The first night of the Billancourt occupation the Renault workers put up a large banner over the factory which said "For higher wages and better pensions". The second day they took it down and put up a new one, which raised the traditional left wing slogan "For a Socialist Party—Communist Party—trade union government". On the third day they took that one down and put up a new banner over the factory, which said "For workers' control of production".

Georges Séguy, long-standing PCF member and leader of the CGT, admitted at a press conference on Friday 17 May, "This general strike is developing without our having called it and it is developing under the responsibility of the workers themselves."

By then every Renault plant was occupied and the occupations were spreading quickly, closing radio, television, airports and fuel supplies. The whole country was paralysed by the biggest general strike in history, with over 10 million taking part.

One of the leaders of the CFDT trade union federation expressed his astonishment:

> In a few days they learnt many things. First of all, that action works... No one thought "the old Man" [de Gaulle] would be beaten on the streets. Pompidou gave in and the students occupied the Sorbonne. On top of this was the power of the demonstration on 13 May; there had been nothing like it since the Liberation. People had never imagined themselves so strong. All the barriers the government had erected against strikes had been broken. For a government employee, it was necessary to give five days' warning before going on strike. The teachers who struck without warning were not sacked. The postal workers struck without warning and the government was incapable of making people respect its laws...there were no lockouts; the employers were frightened of the consequences. The result was workers discovered when you fight well not only is there a chance of winning but the risks involved are quite small.

France ground to halt. Vast swathes of the economy were occupied—all the car plants, virtually the entire aerospace industry, most of engineering across Paris and Normandy and all the shipyards. The occupations spread to the railways, schools, hospitals, the banks and insurance companies, the print industry and the department stores. Workers in museums, art galleries, theatres and film studios all joined the action. The movement included the dancers of the Folies Bergère and film makers withheld their work from the Cannes Film Festival in solidarity. Even the professional football players occupied the headquarters of the French Football Federation.

The Paris correspondent of the *Observer* wrote:

> All over France a calm, obedient, irresistible wave of working class power is engulfing the factories, dockyards, mines, railway depots, bus garages and sorting offices. Trains, mail, and air flights are virtually at a standstill. Production lines in chemicals, steel, metal working, textiles, shipbuilding and a score of other industries have ground to a halt. Nearly a million men and women in key industries are seizing their places of work and closing the gates.

A movement of this magnitude questions who runs society. In Nantes a central strike committee took over the town hall. Road blocks were set up and the committee issued travel permits and petrol coupons. Workers' committees negotiated with local peasants to organise food supply and distribution at reduced prices, while the unions controlled shop prices to prevent profiteering. Committees like this were set up in many communities. As well as practical tasks like dealing with the rubbish they produced leaflets and propaganda.

Workers showed they could take over and run society. For a fortnight at the end of May the regime was in disarray. De Gaulle had ruled with an iron fist. Now he was laughed at. The strikes made it impossible for him to do anything. As Chris Harman explained in his book about 1968, *The Fire Last Time*:

> Indications suggest that the mass of small shopkeepers and businessmen supported de Gaulle. So did most of the prosperous farmers. Among the strikers there were those who passively tolerated the strikes, hoping they would lead to

higher pay, without dropping their right wing or Gaullist ideas. These groups, together with the very rich, may even have been a majority of the population. Yet from 15 to 29 May they were of no consequence.

The government was increasingly isolated with no apparent way out of the dead end in which it found itself. It did have the armed forces and the police. But how far could it rely on them in an all-out confrontation with the mass of workers? Of the 168,000 soldiers, 120,000 were conscripts and some were openly sympathetic with the strikers. The left wing weekly *Nouvel Observateur* reported that after the 5th Army had been put on the alert for strikebreaking, "committees were created ready to turn against their superiors and sabotage transport and armoured cars".

On 15 May the secretary of the police union warned on the radio, "I almost received a mandate at our general meeting to call a strike against the government..." The CRS could still batter the students, as they proved again on the night of 24 May. But an attack on the mass of organised workers was different. If there was any possibility the police might refuse to obey orders, the government dare not take the risk. A police mutiny would have meant final defeat.

De Gaulle derided

So the government was powerless. At the end of the first week of the strikes and occupations de Gaulle broadcast to the country and promised a "referendum on participation" offering to resign if he lost the referendum. He was greeted with derision.

To restore government credibility it was essential to end the strikes, so the day after de Gaulle's broadcast his prime minister, Georges Pompidou, called union leaders and employers together for negotiations. It seemed a deal had been agreed. The Grenelle Agreement conceded a 35 percent increase in the minimum wage and a 7 percent increase in all other wages.

But the union leaders would have to put it to the test of mass meetings in the occupied factories. The first of these meetings was at Renault Billancourt—a CGT stronghold. When two CGT leading officials proposed the agreement they were met with a stony silence and then booing. By contrast, when the leader of the minority CFDT union stressed that the agreement allowed the factory to continue striking for its own local demands he was cheered loudly.

The Renault decision was followed by votes to continue the strikes and occupations at all the major plants and the smaller plants voted to follow the big battalions. Within a day the CGT leaders were calling on workers to fight locally, plant by plant, to win better results than the Grenelle deal. The general strike continued and it looked as if Gaullism was finished.

Depressed, the president fled to Germany on 29 May amid rumours that he had resigned. The world's media talked of "France's May revolution". If the elements of workers' power had been encouraged, then it could have happened. Instead the movement was stifled by its bureaucrats.

The powerful French Communist Party threw away the chance to get rid of de Gaulle and his class for good by convincing workers to hand control back to the bosses on the offer of a general election and major concessions. They simply repeated the Thorez line from 1936: "One must know how to end a strike."

How could such a sudden turnaround happen? Above all else the Communist Party wanted parliamentary influence and it could not achieve that unless it could prove to its potential allies that it commanded substantial working class support. The PCF leadership thought that the best way to do this was by taking command of the strike movement and exercising firm control over it.

Union and party activists were told not simply to support strikes, which were beginning spontaneously, but to take the lead in them. Harman explains:

> They were given a two-fold task; to spread the strike movement but also to control it, to make sure it remained in safe, trade union channels and was not influenced by the revolutionary groups or the radicalised students.
>
> What this meant was shown at Renault Billancourt. Students from the Sorbonne made a "long march" right across Paris to show solidarity and offer support. They were met by row upon row of CGT stewards who barred access to the workers inside the occupied plant. This experience was repeated on a smaller scale in factory after factory. The student struggle might well have inspired the workers' struggle, but the CGT and the PCF were determined not to have revolutionary students influencing "their" workers.

To keep control the union and PCF activists discouraged the mass of ordinary workers from participating in the occupations or from discussing the political issues raised by the sudden upsurge in struggle. Sometimes this didn't work but too often it did.

As one historian of the movement wrote:

> The CGT's most important initial concern in the days after 17 May was to make sure its militants ran as many of the locally elected strike committees as possible. In a minority of cases sit-downs were mass phenomena and did involve a great deal of discussion and debate. But more often than not they were cadre actions, in which whole plants were occupied by skeleton crews of pickets and maintenance workers. In such cases most of the strikers probably stayed at home and observed the crisis unfolding, with sympathy to be sure, on radio and TV. [G Ross, *Workers and Communists in France* (1982)]

Even worse, the CGT leaders did their best to isolate one strike committee from another. For example, Renault Billancourt CGT refused on 23 May to receive a delegation from the occupation at Renault Flins. As a result there was no network of strike committees.

The failure of the Grenelle negotiations to end the strike led all the mainstream politicians to assume that de Gaulle's regime was finished. But the rejection of Grenelle was as big a problem for the leaders of the Communist Party and the union leaders as it was for de Gaulle and Pompidou. The bureaucrats had never intended to topple the government. They merely wanted to use the strikes and occupations as a bargaining tool. Now things were getting out of their control and they panicked.

De Gaulle was persuaded to fight on by the head of the French army in Germany, General Massu, and he returned to France the following day. The Gaullists called for a demonstration of all those who supported the regime and their leader broadcast to the nation on radio and television, announcing that he was holding on to power, by force if necessary, and that he was dissolving parliament and calling a general election.

500,000 of the well to do and right wingers assembled in the Place de la Concorde on the Saturday evening in response to de Gaulle's appeal. That night police tried to break the railway strike by evicting pickets from the stations, but they couldn't force the rail workers back to work.

The real weakness of the regime was now exposed. It was all a huge bluff on de Gaulle's part but the PCF, the trade union leaders and the reformist left in the French Socialist Party never challenged it. They all denounced de Gaulle's speech but they rushed to welcome the elections. The following day CGT leader Séguy announced, "It is in the interests of workers to be able to express their desire for change in the context of elections."

For both the PCF and the CGT preparing for and contesting elections meant ditching the strikes and occupations as quickly as they could. Within three days negotiations were concluded and there was a return to work in the key public services—power, fuel, post and transport. What the police had failed to achieve on the Saturday evening the CGT had managed by the Tuesday.

The decision to end the strikes and occupations in return for an election provoked anger. Thousands demonstrated in Paris chanting, "Election, treason—the fight goes on." There were lots of workers who were opposed to the return to work, and even among those who did go back, some were willing to walk out again. As a trade union official pointed out:

> Despite the money and other difficulties the strike had become like a festival. For two or three weeks the strikers lived in a spirit of total freedom; no employers, no bosses, the hierarchy had disappeared. So before calling the strike off people hesitated.

Unfortunately those militants capable of holding the line against the enormous social weight of the PCF and the CGT were too few and far between and there was no network of strike committees. The revolutionary left was extremely weak at the start of 1968. The Maoist and Trotskyist organisations had less than a thousand members between them. Most were students and hardly any were rooted inside the working class.

The far left grew massively during the May events but this was mainly among students. The PCF and CGT were able, sometimes with great difficulty, to keep the strikes relatively passive and to exclude revolutionary students from the factory occupations.

De Gaulle's regime had been given time to regroup. The occupations were ended and the mass movement was bought off with very substantial economic gains in the form of wages, extra holidays and increased union rights. The Communist Party used everything in its power to get workplaces back to work.

By polling day the revolutionary left was banned and the rank and file was confused and demoralised. The right, who had been terrified by the mass movement, flocked behind "strong man" de Gaulle, and he won the election. Many on the left were shocked by the result, but it proved that workers' confidence can't be turned off and then turned back on again like a tap.

Electoral ambitions of the PCF

The PCF had long since abandoned any attachment to the idea of working class self-emancipation. In the middle of a truly historic struggle its politics led it to promote a contemptible operation. It sacrificed a living movement for electoral ambitions that proved to be out of reach.

But the French May proved that workers' revolt can suddenly erupt, even when the workers themselves least expect it. The events had an enormous impact on the British left. In a major speech at the end of May 1968, Harold Wilson's minister of technology, Tony Benn, spelt out the meaning of the French workers' revolt: "It would be foolish to assume that people will be satisfied for much longer with a system that confines their national political role to the marking of a ballot paper with a single cross once every five years."

In June the newly launched revolutionary newspaper *Black Dwarf* filled its front page with the big, bold headline "We Shall Fight—We Shall Win—Paris, London, Rome, Berlin".

The June 1968 issue of *Socialist Worker* had a special eyewitness account from an International Socialists delegation to France:

> Revolution in the advanced countries is the order of the day. Today France is in turmoil—tomorrow it could be Spain, Britain or Italy. The role played by the students has also become clear. Although they can never be the agents of social change they can act as a catalyst in the process. The activities of the French students provided the flashpoint for the frustrations of the workers; their demands for a new social order voiced the feelings of many workers.

But *Socialist Worker* faced up to the difficulties and the obstacles—notably the grip of reformism and the lack of revolutionary organisation:

> The most serious problem for the French workers is the complete absence of any revolutionary organisation capable of articulating and generalising the mass strike. The field is therefore wide open for the French Communist Party.

The aftermath of 1968

The great events in France were followed in 1969 by the Italian "hot autumn". Spontaneous walkouts and occupations in Italy's big car plants were followed by street demonstrations and clashes with the police.

A year earlier there had been a series of occupations and battles on the Italian campuses and in high schools. In Turin the "hot autumn" was preceded by strikes over wages and housing, which helped unite students and workers, the skilled and unskilled.

A number of left wing groups had sprung up and one of them, Lotta Continua, was strong in Turin. The Fiat Mirafiori car plant there became a focus for its agitation. The workers of Turin and Milan took up the anticapitalist, anti-war slogans of the left wing students.

New forms of organisation emerged as factory councils brought workers together in mass assemblies, electing delegates to represent them regardless of trade union membership. New forms of action were organised: stop and go, work to rule, and internal demonstrations where workers marched through the factories and took them over.

The strike wave continued after the autumn of 1969 and Lotta Continua and three other revolutionary organisations grew from small groups to become parties, each with over 10,000 members and many more supporters.

In 1969 Argentina experienced the Cordobaza—a near uprising as the car workers of Cordoba fought against the military and took over their factories. At the end of May workers from the car and power plants decided to transform their general strike into "an active strike". Columns of workers marched on the centre of Cordoba chasing the police force and taking control of the central area of the city.

5,000 soldiers then forced the workers to retreat and workers occupied their factories. In the fighting and repression that followed workers were killed, but it did not stop the mobilisations. The Cordobaza opened up a three-year period of mass strikes, factory occupations and violent demonstrations.

In November 1970 Chile elected a Popular Unity government with socialist Salvador Allende as president—a reflection of the rising class struggle. Workers seized the land and the factories when the owners and the bosses tried to sabotage the movement for change. Production continued under the control of the trade unions. Out of these struggles workers built their *cordones*—the Chilean equivalent of the workers' councils that arise in every revolutionary crisis.

Yet the Popular Unity government saw workers' aspirations as the chief threat to its existence. Allende called in the army to restore order and return the factories to the bosses. When socialists warned Allende that the ruling class was preparing a coup, he asked the army to investigate. The generals seized the initiative and carried out their brutal counter-revolution in September 1973.

In 1974, six years after the French general strike, class struggle erupted in Portugal, toppling a fascist dictatorship that had ruled since the 1920s. Portugal was the first colonial power in Europe. By 1974 it was losing the war to control its African colonies and its army of 200,000 was eating up half the state budget of what was the poorest country in Europe.

On 25 April sections of the officer corps overthrew the dictator Salazar, triggering an explosion of struggle that created a mass working class movement overnight. This movement prevented the consolidation of a new conservative regime. The defeat of the right deepened radicalisation among the workers and within the army and the navy.

In factories all over Portugal workers' committees were elected. In the big companies and multinationals economic demands went alongside the demand for *saneamento*—the purging of members of the management or administration who had been connected with the fascist regime. The massive shipyards of Lisnave and Setnave were occupied. Miners struck in May for a minimum wage, free medical care, paid holidays and a purge of all managers linked with fascism.

Firestone workers in Lisbon, Alcohete, Porto and Coimbra occupied their factories. Foreign companies like Plessey, Timex and ITT started repatriating capital. They attempted to close down and move out parts of their operations. Workers responded by taking over the factories. In June 3,000 Portuguese airline workers surrounded the company's administration block, trapped the bosses in their offices and demanded settlement of their wage claim.

There was a major struggle over the control of the media, with newspapers and radio stations being occupied under workers' control. Workers organised on a neighbourhood basis to control health, education, housing and transport. In a country where 2 million lived in slums, empty houses belonging to the rich were occupied. In a matter of months workers had put socialist revolution on the agenda.

But while the revolutionary groups and the left within the armed forces movement had pushed things to a point where the old structures of power had nearly disintegrated, they did not have enough influence to overcome the combined influence of the Portuguese Communist and Socialist parties. They were able to put the state structure back together and hold the workers' movement back from taking action. European capitalism breathed a huge sigh of relief.

The French events had a big impact in Britain too. In 1969 working class resistance defeated the rightward moving Labour government's plan to place legal restrictions on shop floor trade unionism. The vicious Tory government elected in 1970 had been routed by mass industrial action by the end of 1973. By February 1974 the Tories were in dire straits. During the miners' strike the government panicked and called a general election under the slogan "Who runs the country?" It lost.

8.

BRITAIN IN THE 1970S: WORKERS ON THE MOVE

> On no previous occasion in British history has the administration of the day suffered such a sequence of reverses from groups of workers.
>
> **—Anthony Barnett, "Class Struggle and the Heath Government", *New Left Review* 77 (Jan/Feb 1973)**

BRITAIN'S FIRST factory occupation was in July 1971 at Upper Clyde Shipbuilders (UCS). It caught the imagination of millions and turned the tide against a Tory government hell-bent on attacking working people.

The UCS work-in came in response to rising unemployment and the decision by the Tory cabinet to impose mass redundancies and close two of the four shipyards in Glasgow. The UCS campaign slogan—"The right to work"—became instantly popular and was adopted by workers everywhere. Regardless of its political limitations, the work-in sparked a wave of militant occupations against redundancies and closures throughout Britain.

The post-war boom, which lasted into the mid-1960s, brought full employment and gave workers enormous self-confidence and bargaining power. In those days the rest of Europe referred to strikes as "the British disease". But until 1971 redundancy was the Achilles heel of an otherwise strong trade union movement.

Harold Wilson's Labour government had introduced the Redundancy Payments Act in 1965. It was deliberately framed to encourage workers and their union

The work-in at Upper Clyde Shipbuilders, 1971.

leaders to accept sackings without a fight. For five years or so it worked. The act weakened resistance by putting the focus on redundancy pay instead of job losses.

Militants who could lead fights on wages and conditions felt impotent in the face of new technology, rationalisation and closures. The demands adopted by the unions—"last in first out", "voluntary redundancy", "early retirement", "natural wastage"—were all defensive and compliant. Strike days rose by 25 percent between 1965 and 1970, but the number of strike days fighting redundancy fell by half, despite the fact that job losses were increasing over this period.

End of the post-war boom

The long post-war boom was ending with a rapid growth in unemployment and a big rise in the number of sackings. The first real attempt at fighting redundancy was in 1969. Faced with 1,700 sackings, workers at GEC's factories in Liverpool voted to occupy. But two days before the occupations were scheduled to kick off, a mass meeting reversed the decision and the redundancies went ahead. Two years elapsed before the idea of occupation reappeared.

If Britain had so far missed out on factory occupations, it certainly made up for it after the summer of 1971. The UCS work-in triggered a wave of more militant occupations against sackings, and most were successful. In early 1972 over 30 factories in Greater Manchester occupied, not over job losses, but as part of the engineers' pay campaign.

Occupations were increasingly used as an offensive tactic to improve wages and conditions and the tactic spread from blue to white collar and public sector workers. These events were part of the powerful mass movement that destroyed the Tory government and terrified the bosses. Royden Harrison writes:

> The labour unrest of 1970-74 was more massive and incomparably more successful than its predecessor of 1910-14. Millions became involved in campaigns of civil disobedience, arising out of resistance to the government's Industrial Relations Act and its Housing Finance Act. Over 200 occupations of factories, offices, workshops and shipyards occurred between 1972 and 1974 alone and many of them attained all or most of their objectives. [Introduction to *The Independent Collier*, 1978]

What distinguishes the early 1970s from the other high points of class struggle in Britain is not just the scale of rebellion or the militant tactics that were adopted, but their stunning success.

Yet the situation in 1970, just before the UCS sit-in, was very similar to now. Capitalism was entering its first real crisis since the Second World War; the US was bogged down in a long, unwinnable war in Vietnam; inflation was rising after a long period of stability; and the long, slow decline of British capitalism had reached a crisis point for the ruling class.

There were other similarities. Unemployment was on the rise and so were racism, immigration controls and the Nazi National Front. Labour lost the election in 1970 because after six years of government it had demoralised its own supporters. The turnout was the lowest in 35 years and the Labour vote slumped by enough for the Tories under Ted Heath to get in.

Heath's manifesto was the most right wing of any government since the 1930s and it set out to break workers' organisation through a combination of increasing unemployment, tough wage controls and anti-union laws.

Initially the Tory onslaught was very successful. Unemployment was forced up sharply; the draconian Industrial Relations Act was introduced while the TUC did nothing; and wage controls were imposed after the government inflicted defeat on the power workers and then the postal workers in their first national strike.

The fight at UCS

It was the struggle at Upper Clyde Shipbuilders that turned the tide. When the UCS workers took over the shipyards in July 1971, they were the first group to defy the Tory anti-union laws, which had come into force a week before.

Tory industry minister Sir John Davies had made it clear that mass sackings were on the cards when he announced in February 1971 that no money would be made available to "lame ducks" like UCS. In June he refused a request for a £6 million government loan from the UCS management, forcing the consortium to go bust.

On 24 June 100,000 workers in Glasgow stopped work and 50,000 marched through the city demanding the government step in and save the jobs at UCS. There were large delegations from every factory in the west of Scotland and from England too. It was the biggest march in Glasgow since the general strike of 1926.

Undaunted, Davies rose in the House of Commons on 29 July to confirm the sackings and force UCS into receivership. Two of the four yards were to close and 6,000 of the 8,500 jobs would go immediately. Another 40,000 workers whose jobs depended on the yards were in peril. Unemployment on Clydeside was 40 percent up on the previous year. People feared it was the end of shipbuilding in Glasgow.

The next day the workers—led by the UCS Joint Shop Stewards, under the political control of Communists Jimmy Reid and Jimmy Airlie, took over the four yards. The stewards opted for a "work-in" rather than a sit-in. This meant cooperating with the receiver to finish the ships under construction. Concerned primarily with winning public opinion, the work-in was conceived as a Scottish popular front and not a confrontation with government.

Yet UCS workers were demanding "the right to work" not just in words but in deed. Their work-in signalled a change of mood: that redundancy was neither inevitable nor acceptable. Their action raised the hopes of thousands of militants. UCS became a symbol and a focus for all those who wanted to get rid of the Tories.

The initial response from other workers was stunning. On 10 August a meeting in Glasgow of 1,200 shop stewards from every major factory in the west of Scotland backed the work-in, agreed to weekly workplace collections and called a second one-day solidarity strike.

A week later 200,000 Scottish workers struck in support of UCS and 80,000 marched to a rally on Glasgow Green. The government was thrown on the defensive and Strathclyde's chief constable phoned Downing Street to warn that any attempt to use force against the work-in would mean the police could not guarantee order on the streets of Glasgow.

Tory cabinet minister Peter Walker later admitted, "There was a genuine feeling that unless some action was taken social disorder of a type not seen in this country could take place in Glasgow." So the work-in was allowed to continue unmolested. It captured the public mood and the whole labour and trade union bureaucracy were forced to back it.

Regular levies and collections were organised in thousands of workplaces. Financial support flooded in from trade unions across Britain and all over the world. Donations poured in from individuals. One card came with a bouquet of red roses and a cheque for £1,000. The message read "Power to the People, with love from John and Yoko".

In February 1972 the Tories were forced to announce a £35 million government package to save three of the four yards. The struggle continued until October, when the remaining yard was taken over by an American company.

The work-in ended 15 months after it started. Concessions were made on demarcation and the yards were kept open with a reduced workforce. But the Tories had been forced into a humiliating U-turn. It was the government which was left looking like a lame duck.

Despite its many limitations the work-in was seen at the time as an important turning point and a beacon of resistance. *International Socialism* journal wrote at the time:

> Whatever the outcome its significance is that the workers did not accept redundancies or management's right to declare them. Now every group menaced with the prospect of unemployment is prepared to discuss new forms of resistance. Despite its leaders' efforts to confine the struggle, there is no doubt the ideas raised by UCS will spread within the movement.

200 occupations

UCS inspired other, more militant sit-ins. First was the occupation of the Plessey torpedo plant in the Vale of Leven, near Glasgow. It was a smaller workforce with a big percentage of women. Faced with total closure, they launched a full-blooded occupation. They never considered a work-in because there was no work. They refused to allow machinery to be moved. Other Plessey factories pledged blacking (agreeing not to handle or move goods and equipment) and the local community rallied round too.

Just as the Plessey workers were inspired by UCS, so Plessey inspired others. In Birmingham a two-day occupation forced British Leyland to withdraw 900 sackings at Fisher Pressed Steel.

There then followed occupations at the River Don Steelworks and Snow's in Sheffield; Norton Villiers Triumph in Meriden near Coventry; BSA in Birmingham; BL Cowley; Allis Chalmers in north Wales; Sexton Shoes in Fakenham; St Helen's Plastics in Lancashire; Gardiners Engines and Lawrence Scotts, both in Manchester; Bryant Colour Printing, Baynard's Press, Stanmore Engineering and Seiko Time, all in London; Thorneycroft's in Basingstoke; Harris Engineering in Turnbridge Wells; McLaren Controls in Glasgow; and many, many more.

There were over 200 occupations between 1972 and 1974. The Fisher-Bendix occupation at Kirkby on Merseyside was one of the most impressive.

In the summer of 1971 a nine-week strike at Fisher-Bendix had halted sackings, but the Thorn Group announced they would close the plant by May 1972. The shop stewards prepared for a fight. One of them described what happened:

> In West Lancashire a large number of well-attended "Support UCS" meetings had been held, largely on the initiative of the International Socialists. They'd spread the idea of a fight against unemployment and a campaign of demos and marches was building up in the area. A delegation of stewards was sent to UCS... We decided a work-in was OK for a public relations job like UCS but it wouldn't do for a serious fight...
>
> Links were established with other plants in the Thorn empire and with local factories and building sites. Plans were laid for preventing the movement of machinery and for future blacking. We collected a 50p weekly levy from every member of the workforce to build a fighting fund. As the management deadline for the first redundancies in January 1972 drew near, the feeling hardened.

A group of militants met to organise a protest inside the plant. They marched to the main administration building and other workers joined them on the way. En route they collected the master keys for the entire factory. Eventually around 200 workers burst into the boardroom and confronted their bosses.

The shop stewards' convenor told management to leave the boardroom and reconsider their closure decision. He gave them ten minutes to do so. The managers sheepishly consented and came back ten minutes later to say they were very sorry, but they could not reverse the closure. The workers evicted them and took control of the factory.

A mass meeting of the 800 workers was held immediately. The convenor told them, "Better we occupy, to control from within rather than stand out in the rain and the cold, the fog and the wind, trying to stop scab lorries." They voted unanimously to occupy the factory.

The level of rank and file involvement was impressive. Financial support flooded in and the dockers refused to handle all Thorn products. There was a solidarity strike across Merseyside in support of Fisher Bendix. It linked with the miners' strike and with the unofficial national docks strike. It looked like it might escalate into a general fight against all redundancies.

Following the intervention of local MP Harold Wilson a new company, IPD, agreed to keep the plant open. The victory showed the advantage of an occupation based on a combination of preparation and spontaneity. In four weeks it had set Liverpool ablaze, terrifying both employers and government.

It also inspired a wave of sit-ins in the engineering factories across Greater Manchester.

The pattern of struggle in 1972 was one of victory for our side, with one exception—the national engineering pay claim. Negotiations with the employers collapsed in

January 1972 when the miners' strike was in full swing.

The AUEW engineering union was big and powerful. It had a left executive and a left president, Hugh Scanlon. A national strike alongside the miners would have blown the employers away. Incredibly Scanlon and the executive chose to fight on a local, plant by plant basis. Greater Manchester was the only area where a real fight in support of the claim was organised.

Inspired by events at Fisher Bendix, 30 factories in the area were occupied by thousands of workers in retaliation for employers' lockouts. But these became token sit-ins. Instead of using the occupations to motivate and mobilise thousands of workers, the left officials killed off any attempt to spread the dispute and ensured the sit-ins stayed passive and docile.

It was a missed opportunity for the left. Boredom set in and the movement ebbed away as plants settled individually. Key elements of the wage claim, like a cut in hours and equal pay, were ditched by the union.

Manchester showed the danger of top-down token gestures and proved that sitting in by itself is not enough. Occupations have to become centres of activity. Delegations have to go out and campaign for solidarity. That way the seizure of the workplace provides a base for extending the struggle. Momentum and audacity are the keys to success. Passivity and boredom spell defeat.

The fiasco of the engineers' pay claim was a blip that did not stem the rising tide. Sit-ins continued right into Harold Wilson's Labour government, which won the "Who runs the country?" election, called by an embattled Ted Heath during the second miners' strike in February 1974.

Labour in office

The fall of the Heath government gave rise to another upsurge of struggle, culminating in a wave of unofficial strikes which paralysed central Scotland in the winter of 1974/75. At first Labour had no choice but to go along with the pay explosion that followed the collapse of Heath's incomes policy. Tom Jackson, right wing leader of the postal workers, put it very well when he likened the incoming Labour government to "the owner of a giant Las Vegas slot machine that has suddenly got stuck in favour of the customers".

In his 1975 book, *The Crisis*, Tony Cliff pointed out:

> There has probably never been a period like the present in Britain for the sheer variety of working class struggle. Factory occupations have mushroomed, not only to resist closure, but also in the fight for higher wages, bonus payments, equal pay, against victimisation and against racism.

Here is a list of just some of the occupations covered in *Socialist Worker* during 1974-76:

Ruston Paxman Diesels, Wigan, 100 workers for reinstatement of shop steward; Charles McNeil Engineering, Glasgow, 120 workers for wages; Punfield & Barlow, NW London, 200 Pakistani AUEW members for better wages; Dresser Europe factory, Bracknell, Berkshire, 150 workers for bonus payments; Hick Hargreaves, Bolton, 250 workers for higher wages; Kodak Hemel Hempstead, 1,000 workers for union recognition; Plessey Telecoms, Beeston, 6,000 workers for higher wages; Coles Cranes, Darlington, 200 workers for higher wages; Adwest engineering, Reading, 400 workers to stop closure; Strachan Engineering Eastleigh, 70 workers opposing closure; SEI Instruments, Heywood, Lancs, 400 women for equal pay; Imperial Typewriters, Hull, 200 women workers against factory closure; Brookes Cylinders, Jarrow, 150 workers against closure; Educational Audio Visual, 40 NUJ members against redundancy; Hammersmith Hospital, W London,

400 NHS workers for pay increase; Persona Razor Blades, Glasgow, 300 workers for a wage increase; Triumph, Coventry, 1,100 white collar staff for pay regrading; Magnesium Elektron, Manchester, 500 women workers for wage rise; Lawson Paragon Printing Group factories at Bury St Edmunds, Sunderland, Wellingborough, St Neots, Portsmouth, Gainsborough and Birkenhead, 1,500 print workers sitting in for a pay rise; Smith Hutton Shipyard, Dundee, 400 workers against closure; GEC Elliot's, S London, 70 workers for pay parity with other GEC plants; Cammell Laird, Birkenhead, 150 contract workers against redundancy; Ford Swansea, 200 workers against redundancy; Howard Rotovators, Halesworth, Suffolk, 150 workers against short-time working; Massey Ferguson, 5,000 workers for a wage rise; Crossfield Electronics, London, 350 workers against redundancy; P&O Sealink, Basingstoke, 110 workers against redundancy; Prestwich Hospital, Manchester, 150 staff over grading issues; GEC, Tottenham, plant occupied twice for reinstatement of victimised stewards; Rolls Royce, Blantyre, Glasgow, 500 workers occupy for 20 weeks against closure; Courtaulds, Skelmersdale, 800 workers against speed-ups and for taking on more workers; BP, Grangemouth, 1,700 workers over pensions and fringe benefits; council nursery, Dundee, staff occupy against closure; Hopkinson's, Huddersfield, 200 workers over wages.

But it soon became clear that Labour's election victory had blunted the political edge of the industrial struggle, and with the support of left wing union leaders Jack Jones and Hugh Scanlon, the Labour government was eventually able to impose wage controls, which survived until the "winter of discontent" in 1978-79.

Labour's Social Contract, crafted by a joint TUC/ Labour Party committee, brought the biggest fall in real wages for a generation. When the deepening world recession led to a doubling of unemployment, militancy collapsed and strikes fell to their lowest level since the 1950s.

The trade union leaders' allegiance to Labour and the lack of generalisation meant struggles became increasingly isolated and more dependent on the officials. A classic example was the occupation at Imperial Typewriters in Hull. What began as a daring takeover by 200 women facing the sack was stifled and controlled by their trade union officials and ended in defeat. The officials barred outsiders and the occupation never got beyond its own four walls.

Other groups fighting redundancy were sidetracked into workers' co-operatives—like Norton Villiers Triumph in Birmingham, KME on Merseyside and the *Scottish Daily Express* in Glasgow. Cabinet minister Tony Benn was enthusiastic, offering the NVT workers' co-operative £5 million. A similar offer was made to the workers on the *Scottish Daily Express* to help with the launch of the *Scottish Daily News* co-operative.

Naturally, groups facing redundancy saw the workers' co-operative as a radical way out of their difficulties. They were wrong. To survive in a competitive market, the workers had to drive themselves much harder than they ever did under their old bosses. As an editorial in *Socialist Worker* pointed out:

> You cannot build islands of socialism in a sea of capitalism. Workers' management of a commercial concern operating in that sea deprives the workers of the strength of union organisation directed against management.

The print unions worried that the *Scottish Daily News* would undermine the resistance to sackings in other newspapers. The *Express* had employed 2,000 in

Glasgow, while the new paper needed only 500. It made the manning levels of other newspapers look bloated.

The occupation of a factory is a tactic of class struggle—not an experiment in workers' control. Workers' control cannot exist in a single factory. In 1975 a shop steward wrote a letter to *Socialist Worker* explaining why:

> The co-op means workers are landed with the responsibility of making the place a going concern. It means lowering wages and increasing productivity. It absolves the government and the employers from responsibility and it solves the receiver's problem. Labour has tried to turn workers away from demanding nationalisation—the co-op formula allows them to do this and sound radical.

Until 1974 the Communist Party played a dual role, initiating actions like UCS but seeking to limit them and keep them under control. After Labour came to office the CP played a negative role, blocking rank and file initiatives like the National Rank and File Movement and the Right to Work Campaign. Because of its reluctance to criticise or break from the left union leaders, it opposed unofficial strikes against the Social Contract wage controls.

Unfortunately, the level of political organisation lagged behind the scale of the struggle. The revolutionary left had grown but it was too small to counter the influence of reformism on the working class movement. The feeling among a growing minority, that workers had the power to run society, began to ebb away, and there was a general shift to the right.

Jonathan Neale recalls a key moment in these events:

> In 1974 the new Labour government presided over mass unemployment, a wage freeze, hospital closures and cuts.

> The trade union leaders and the Communist Party said we had to support the Labour government, because at least they weren't Tories. I was in the Socialist Workers Party then. We only had 4,000 members, mostly recruited after 1968, but we meant it about socialism from below.
>
> In 1976 I was a shop steward in a London hospital. I went to a conference called by the shop stewards in the car plants in Birmingham. They were led by Communists. They wanted us to reject the "Social Contract" with Labour because they were under pressure from below with car workers losing their jobs. But they didn't want us to support the skilled tool-room workers who were on unofficial strike at British Leyland against the wage freeze—because they really wanted us to do what Labour needed. I learned then don't listen to the leaders' words; just watch if they support every struggle.
>
> I learned another thing. The SWP at that conference argued for supporting the tool-room workers. We lost the vote, about 1,000 to 700. We lost it because the Communist Party and the reformists had built more and longer in the big workplaces than we had... I had learned that we needed an organisation of socialists committed to power from below.

Occupations and sit-ins continued until the end of the Labour government. Prominent examples included Smiths Industries, Cricklewood, in London; Essex International at Kilwinning in Ayrshire; Chloride in Dagenham; Plessey in Kirkby; Drylanders in St Helens; and GEC, Coventry.

But the numbers steadily dwindled until they were few and far between, proof of how much the movement had retreated under Labour. All of this meant that when there was a revival of struggle towards the end of the Labour government during the "winter of discontent", it was bitter, sectional and did not lead to the generalisation that had taken place in the early 1970s under the Tories.

But there was no doubting the collective power of the British working class and the capacity of ordinary workers to grow in struggle. 1972 marks a high point in working class history. Paul Foot described it as "the year when the massed ranks of organised capital crumbled under the mighty weight of workers' power".

9.

BRITAIN: RESISTANCE IN THE DOWNTURN

BY THE 1980s the balance of class forces had shifted dramatically from the heady days of 1972. It is not Margaret Thatcher who deserves the credit for this turnaround. The real damage was inflicted by the Wilson-Callaghan Labour governments, with the considerable help of the trade union leaders.

Thatcher inherited and extended Labour's anti-union policies and the "monetarism" that began under Harold Wilson's successor, Jim Callaghan, and his chancellor, Dennis Healey. Some of the achievements claimed for Thatcher were real; some are not.

She did force the working class movement even further onto the defensive, and she did manage to inflict a very serious defeat on the miners, from which the movement is still recovering.

Her acolytes in the media wanted working people to believe that she had crushed the unions. She certainly tried, but she failed. Even her biggest victory was won at a terrible cost to the ruling class. The year-long war waged on the miners turned out to be a pyrrhic victory.

Despite all the propaganda to the contrary, the Thatcher years saw ordinary working people resist and win some significant victories at the expense of her class. Workplace occupations never disappeared off the radar even in the grimmer moments of the 1980s and 1990s.

There were a number of important sit-ins and occupations, which encouraged resistance and inspired great

Lee Jeans workers during their seven month-long factory occupation in 1981.

acts of solidarity from other groups of workers. Some notable examples include Meccano and Massey Ferguson in Liverpool; Gardner's Engines and Lawrence Scott Engineering, both in Manchester; Lawrence Scott Engineering, Norwich; Plessey's in Swindon; British Printing Corporation and the *Camden Journal*, both in London; Bennett Brothers, Ashton Under Lyme; Stone Platt Machines in Oldham; Plansee Engineering in South Yorkshire; Lee Jeans in Greenock; Bestobell Insulation in Glasgow; British Leyland, Bathgate; Timex in Dundee; Staffa in East London; British Aluminium at Invergordon; Lovable Bras, Cumbernauld; Caterpillar in Uddingston, near Glasgow; Kvaerner in Clydebank; and Glacier RPB in Glasgow.

Some ended in outright or partial victory and that was no mean feat at that time. The rest of this chapter looks at four of these occupations to see what they can teach us for present and future battles.

Gardner's, Manchester

The occupation of the Gardner's engine factory in Manchester in October 1980 was an immensely important struggle. A group of workers had at last taken a stand against a wave of closures and redundancies that were destroying jobs at the rate of 3,000 a day.

Gardner's helped galvanise the movement of opposition to Thatcher that built the huge Labour Party protest marches against unemployment in Liverpool and Glasgow in the winter of 1980-81.

It was not the first occupation under the Thatcher government—there had been occupations at Meccano and Massey Ferguson in Liverpool—but Gardner's was by far the biggest and it won after a three-month struggle that lasted over Christmas.

Gardner's was part of the Hawker-Syddeley group. It had a strong tradition of union organisation and socialist politics. There was a 13-week sit-in during 1973 that ended in victory. Significantly in the late 1970s Anti Nazi League leaflets were distributed at the factory gates by the shop stewards because they wanted to make it clear to all union members where they stood on the question of racism.

When the shop stewards lodged a wage claim in September 1980, management refused to make any offer unless the workforce accepted 700 redundancies and a restriction on the role of the shop stewards.

Faced with an attack on wages, conditions and jobs, a mass meeting voted to occupy and take over the factory to stop any job losses, protect conditions and get a decent wage rise.

The occupation was a lesson in democracy and membership involvement. Its impact could be seen from the fantastic response Gardner's workers received as they toured the country to sustain their occupation. Collections were organised in all the Clydeside shipyards and engineering plants and there were collections for the occupation in every colliery in south Wales.

Gardner's had pride of place on the 80,000-strong demonstration against unemployment that marched through Liverpool in November 1980. Up and down the country groups of unemployed workers organised factory gate collections for Gardner's through the Right to Work Campaign, and this helped spread support and publicity for the occupation.

The Manchester districts of the engineering union organised weekly levies of all of their 100,000 members in support of the occupation. The Sheffield district took the unprecedented step of organising a weekly levy of its members for Gardner's—a struggle that was outside its own district.

The dispute dragged on, but the determination of

the workforce and the massive level of funds raised from other trade unionists around the country were high enough to sustain the occupation and wear down the management. The Gardner's victory showed that workers could fight and win against a background of high unemployment.

Lee Jeans, Greenock

It is not always the strongest groups of workers who fight back. In February 1981 the working class movement in Scotland suffered a terrible blow when a mass meeting of workers at the giant Talbot Linwood car plant near Glasgow rejected a shop stewards committee recommendation to occupy the plant and prevent its closure and the loss of 6,000 jobs.

Hopes were buried of a decisive struggle against unemployment, which could have aroused the whole of Clydeside as UCS had done ten years earlier. Linwood had a deserved reputation as the most militant factory in the west of Scotland and an occupation there would have commanded massive support. Instead the factory was closed without a fight.

At the same time 240 women clothing workers at Lee Jeans in Greenock began an occupation of their factory, which was threatened with closure. Most of the workers were teenagers with no experience of struggle or trade unions.

Lee Jeans was owned by an American multinational, Vanity Fare, and the Greenock factory was one of 40 they owned worldwide. Vanity Fare decided to close Greenock and move the work and the machinery to their Irish plant.

They reckoned without the workers, who fought as if their lives depended on it. In a Clydeside shipyard town with over 16 percent unemployment, there was no future outside the factory for its young female workforce. One 20 year old occupier had already been made redundant five times.

The occupation lasted for seven months, and rank and file organisation was crucial to its success. The National Union of Tailoring and Garment Workers only officially recognised the dispute after six weeks and did precious little else to help their members.

But the strikers were able to win fantastic solidarity, and socialists played a crucial role in making the political arguments and providing the networks to deliver it. Thousands of collection sheets were distributed and local shipyard shop stewards helped set up a trade union support committee. Delegations from the occupation toured workplaces around the country—a move initiated by the SWP, along with nationwide pickets of Vanity Fare shops and outlets.

The bosses got a court order to evict the women from the factory. On the appointed day 1,000 workers came from the shipyards, engineering plants and coal mines to surround the factory and defend the occupation.

British and Irish dockers refused to move any of the company's goods. And even though their own union withdrew official support, in the end the occupation stopped the closure of the factory and saved 140 jobs.

Caterpillar: the revenge of the pink panther

Even occupations that lose can make a big difference.

In January 1987 the US based multinational Caterpillar called a press conference in the Holiday Inn in Glasgow, to announce the shock closure of its profitable Uddingston plant, with the loss of all 1,200 jobs.

The local shop stewards got wind of the bosses' press conference and gatecrashed it. To management's embarrassment, the union convenor stood up, interrupted Caterpillar's American boss and in a loud voice told the assembled press, radio and TV cameras that the factory was now occupied under workers' control and that it would stay occupied until all the jobs were saved. It was the main item that evening on the TV news bulletins.

So began a 104-day occupation that proved a marvellous example of workers' ingenuity and solidarity. The occupation came two years after the miners' defeat and the damage done to the movement was there for all to see. The leadership of the AUEW did not lift a finger to help win the blacking of Caterpillar that would have forced a climb-down from the company. Yet despite the cowardice of their own union leaders the workers mounted a terrific fight. They defied the law, stayed solid and won a fantastic level of support throughout the working class.

Uddingston was an old mining town and unemployment in the local area was 19 percent. There had been a spate of other local closures and redundancies either side of Christmas, including the nearby Gartcosh steelworks.

The closure of Caterpillar ranks as one of the most callous management decisions ever. Only days before the announcement the Tory minister for Scotland, Malcolm Rifkind, had lavished praise on Caterpillar as "an example of the kind of multinational that Scotland needs".

Weeks earlier the company had announced, in a blaze of publicity, a massive £63 million investment in the plant, guaranteeing its long term future as the site chosen to produce the company's new model. The sudden change of plan provoked a bitter response and workers seized the plant.

The public campaign mounted by the workforce meant they were able to raise over £20,000 a week, every week, to sustain the occupation. Delegations toured Britain and spoke to virtually every major factory in the UK. Caterpillar was a beacon of resistance for a dispirited movement.

The role played by a few socialist shop stewards and the influence of *Socialist Worker*, which had been sold inside the plant week in, week out since the early 1970s, were significant. The occupation looked outwards from day one. It sought and won support internationally. Shop stewards travelled to Belgium and France to set up links with Caterpillar shop stewards there, and the action won praise and support from Caterpillar workers in the US, who were also under attack.

The French and Belgian plants held a token stoppage in support of Uddingston and threatened to go on indefinite strike if Caterpillar tried to evict the Uddingston workers. And despite the cowardice of the AUEW executive, dockers and lorry drivers imposed unofficial blacking on the movement of Caterpillar goods.

Although the workforce were mainly male, their strong involvement in the year-long miners' strike taught them the importance of setting up a women's support group. It proved crucial in holding the occupation together and in winning mass support for the occupation in the local communities.

There was a local march of 10,000 in support of the occupation. Every week large groups of Caterpillar workers and their supporters organised street collections in Glasgow and throughout the industrial towns of Lanarkshire.

The two local football teams played a benefit match to raise money for the occupation and thousands of pounds were collected at every Celtic and Rangers football match in nearby Glasgow. In every major town in Scotland there was a Caterpillar Occupation Support Group.

The decision of the workforce to build the "Pink Panther" during the occupation was a masterstroke. This was directed to the outside world to underline the desperate need in the so-called "underdeveloped countries" for the type of earth-moving equipment built at Uddingston.

So the sit-in became a "work-in" to show the world what Caterpillar workers could produce, and the "Pink Panther" was born. It was a giant tractor assembled by the workers and painted pink to clearly distinguish it from the usual Caterpillar yellow. The workers agreed to donate it free to Scottish War on Want, in defiance of Caterpillar US. The machine had a serious purpose. The new banner hung over the front of the factory summed it up: "Cat Workers Say: We Can, and We Will, Help to 'Feed the World'."

Eventually the Pink Panther was driven, in the full glare of the media, the ten miles into George Square in Glasgow, where it was parked prominently throughout the occupation. Caterpillar got an injunction to prevent it being handed over to War on Want. George Galloway, then the head of the charity, issued a statement: "The tractor will remain in George Square as a very pink, public testimony to the actions of a very mean-spirited multinational."

The Chain Gang was a group of young musicians from different popular bands who got together in April 1987 to record a charity single—"Makin Tracks"—supporting the Caterpillar workers' occupation. The text on the back of the record jacket reads:

> This record was originally written and recorded by Scottish musicians in support of the Caterpillar workers' occupation of their factory in Uddingston, Lanarkshire. The brave occupation hammered home the strength of Scottish workers in their fight to save jobs from multinational madness. The struggle goes on. The profit from this record will go to the War on Want organisation as requested by the Caterpillar Occupation Committee at the controversial end of their sit-in. All the musicians and studio services are given free of charge.

In the end the occupation was sold out by the leaders of the main union, the right wing led Amalgamated Engineering Union (AEU). In February 1987 Caterpillar were granted a legal interdict against the sit-in. The shop stewards argued for defiance and a mass meeting voted by a narrow majority to continue the sit-in, despite the right wing EETPU electricians' union ending its support and its members leaving the occupation.

The company announced it would not use the legal interdict to evict the occupiers and regain the factory immediately, but expected the AEU to issue a formal instruction to their members to end the action. Jimmy Airlie, the Communist who led the UCS work-in of 1971, and now the AEU regional full time official in charge of Caterpillar, urged the shop stewards to end the sit-in. They refused and attacked him as a traitor.

The occupation ended in April 1987 when Gavin Laird (subsequently called "Give-in" Laird) and Bill Jordan, leaders of the AEU, threatened to disown the occupation and end all support for it.

In last ditch negotiations with the company the stewards forced a stay of execution and only agreed a return to work on the basis that employment would continue until October 1987 with no compulsory redundancies until after that date; an enhanced redundancy package; and the formation of a working party charged with finding a new owner and saving some of the jobs.

On that basis the massively popular occupation, which raised a fighting fund of £340,000, ended with a return to work at the end of April. The Caterpillar sit-in was one the reasons why the Tories lost most of their Scottish seats despite winning the 1987 general election.

Glacier RPB Glasgow

In November 1996 workers at the Glacier engineering factory at Polmadie, Glasgow, occupied against sackings.

Glacier, part of a multinational car components firm, had sacked its entire Glasgow workforce after they refused to accept new unsafe working practices, changes to their contracts, a reduction in their wages and an attack on union organisation.

Instead of walking out on strike, the 103 workers occupied the plant and locked out the management. Two years earlier they had been locked out themselves after taking strike action. This time they decided to turn the tables on their bosses.

They defied the law and won widespread solidarity for their struggle. With the help of local socialists they toured workplaces to win financial support and organised a solidarity march of 3,000 supporters through the local area. They maintained the occupation over Christmas and workers' families had a party inside the plant on Christmas Day.

Management caved in and the workers won a complete victory. Every job was saved, existing conditions were protected and management were forced to give a written commitment that any future changes would be negotiated and agreed with the union. It was a stunning victory achieved by a small group of workers against a multinational company. And they celebrated the victory by marching back into work under their engineering union banner.

Hungry for information; in front of the free printing press during the Lenin shipyards occupation, Gdansk, Poland 1980.

10.

STRUGGLE, POLITICS AND ORGANISATION

> Revolution is necessary not only because the ruling class cannot be overthrown in any other way but also because only in a revolution can the class which overthrows it rid itself of the accumulated rubbish of the past and become capable of reconstructing society anew.
>
> **—Karl Marx and Frederick Engels, *The German Ideology***

WORKPLACE OCCUPATIONS and sit-in strikes are back as part of a new wave of resistance. More groups of workers are taking militant action, which is often all-out, unofficial and sometimes in defiance of the law. This return of effective workplace militancy is undermining the commonly held view that has prevailed in one form or another since the defeats of the 1980s and 1990s—that industrial action can't win.

Initially workers in Britain were slow in responding to the recession, compared to other European countries. At the beginning of 2009 30,000 workers lost their jobs as Woolworths closed without a fight.

Then in February, when workers' anger at unemployment did boil over into wildcat strikes involving over 10,000 construction workers, it was misdirected against foreign workers. The slogan "British jobs for British workers"—first used by Gordon Brown and then promoted by Derek Simpson of the Unite union during the construction workers' dispute—was xenophobic and divisive.

A Labour prime minister and a prominent trade union leader encouraging groups of workers to wave the union jack and blame "foreigners" for stealing their jobs could only play into the hands of the bosses and the Nazi BNP. It was no surprise when Nazi führer Nick Griffin used Brown's terrible slogan to win votes and recruits in the European election campaign. As Chris Harman wrote:

> Supporters of the existing system believe they can survive any crisis, however much it hurts millions of people, through a mixture of lies, minuscule bribes and threats. The lies will be that someone other than capitalism is responsible for the loss of jobs—the worker in a Chinese sweatshop, the Polish plumber and the refugees from a war instigated by the US.

To fight sackings and the race to the bottom we need to defend all workers, no matter where they come from. The politics of unity and solidarity are critical to any successful movement of resistance. Anti-racism and internationalism are not luxuries.

Socialists and union activists were able to combat and eliminate the "British jobs for British workers" slogan during the second wave of construction strikes, which scored a stunning victory in June. But this is an argument that will not go away so long as capitalism exists.

The more workers struggle and win, the more they reject racism and embrace internationalism.

The great events covered in this pamphlet all show that when the working class moves into struggle it begins to transform itself and the world around it.

We saw that process at work in Britain during the early 1970s when a powerful mass movement toppled a Tory government and terrified the ruling class to the extent that in December 1973 Tory cabinet minister for industry John Davies told his family, "We must enjoy this Christmas for it may be our last one."

The strong shop stewards movement that broke the Heath government is no more, but as new struggles develop it will be possible to forge a new movement based on rank and file resistance. For that to happen, socialists will have to throw themselves into the developing struggles and fight to shape them. If the revival is to grow it will require a much wider political vision.

The collapse of organised reformism within the working class movement and the failure of the left to fill the political vacuum means we have to build a bridge between industrial militancy and the struggle for socialism.

In some respects revolutionaries are better placed to do so than in the early 1970s or at any time since. The insanity and obscenity of capitalism stands more exposed than ever. Loyalty to the Labour Party among rank and file workers has slumped and the Communist Party is no longer the obstacle it was all those years ago.

A new working class

Capitalism is dynamic and has changed the shape of the working class in Britain quite dramatically since the early 1970s. The new working class is enriched by a greater diversity and by a much deeper political radicalisation than was the case 40 years ago at the start of the last great upsurge of struggle.

Britain still has a sizeable group of manufacturing workers with a tradition of organisation. But a new working class is in the making and it is increasingly young, female and multicultural. It includes supermarket workers, airport workers, immigrant catering and cleaning workers, and call centre workers. The companies that employ them are important for British capital.

They make massive profits but they are vulnerable to collective action.

Like the leaders of the American craft unions during the 1930s, union officialdom seems unable or unwilling to organise these new groups. Despite what happened in history our leaders, with a few notable exceptions, claim that the unions cannot recover their muscle until some government is persuaded to pass legislation to increase workers' rights. But as Trotsky once pointed out, "Leaders who wish to begin only when everything is ready are not needed by the working class."

That is not how it happened in the East End of London in 1888 when a strike by the young match girls at Bryant & May triggered the New Unionism; or in the US in the mid-1930s where the unions were built and real gains won through mass struggle initiated by the newest or least organised groups of workers.

The trade union leaders

The unions were built by workers as a bulwark against the capitalist system. But all the great events covered in this book show that one of the biggest obstacles workers have to overcome whenever they fight back is union officialdom.

The decision by the leaders of the CWU in December 2009 to halt the national post strikes and enter talks with management is just one recent example of how trade union leaders throw away the momentum built up by the rank and file. Confining the class struggle within the limits of capitalism presumes that the interests of labour and capital can be reconciled. The leaked documents show that Royal Mail management don't share this presumption.

Trade unions were formed to resist the effects of capitalist exploitation, not to abolish it. And while capitalist democracy permits the development of working class organisation it also seeks to contain and incorporate it. The formation of a conservative labour bureaucracy is inherent in the very nature of trade unionism.

Over 35 years ago Tony Cliff wrote:

> The trade union bureaucracy is a distinct, basically conservative, social formation. Like the god Janus it has two faces. It balances between the employers and the workers. Its fear of mass struggle is much greater than its abhorrence of state control of the unions. At all decisive moments the union bureaucracy is bound to side with the state, but in the meantime it vacillates.

The superior lifestyles of the top officials reflect the circles they move in. They mediate, bargain and compromise. Beatrice and Sydney Webb, Labour supporters and authors of the famous *History of Trade Unionism 1666-1920*, wrote approvingly of the emerging union bureaucracies at the end of the 19th century:

> During these years we watch a shifting of the leadership in the trade union world from the casual enthusiast and irresponsible agitator to a class of salaried officers expressly chosen out of the rank and file of trade unionists for their superior business capacity.

This layer has grown massively since then. Its role is to negotiate with the employers and the government. But negotiation—finding a solution that is acceptable to two sides in conflict—is an entirely different matter from organising to win.

Full time officials are free from the daily grind of work, bullying bosses and job insecurity. When a workplace closes the officials don't get the sack. In the course of struggle workers often come to challenge the wages system. The trade union official, however, depends on its continuation because his or her role is to mediate between employers and workers.

Being determines consciousness. For the bureaucrat struggle appears as a disruption to the bargaining process—a nuisance and an inconvenience. Strikes might break the law and threaten the accumulated funds of the union. Organisation becomes an end in itself.

Trade unionism plays a dual role: a weapon used by sections of workers to defend and improve their conditions; and a means of control over workers' struggle by the labour leaders in the interest of class collaboration. This duality is ever-present, but the balance fluctuates depending on the forces involved and the actual course of the struggle. The bureaucracy is not all-powerful. Its normal role is one of balancing—of seeking a deal within the framework of the system and preferably one that is favourable to the workers concerned.

Officials don't usually set out to lose disputes. They want a compromise without risking a general confrontation. The trade union leaders are not workers—but neither are they bosses. They depend on working class organisation and without it they are impotent. Their power stems from their ability to defend members, negotiate improvements and protect their base. They seek to defend it in their own fashion—limited, sectional and collaborationist—but to defend it nonetheless.

Saying that "officials always sell out" is too crude. Trade union leaders can lead real struggles and whether they do so or not isn't determined by their own thoughts or attitudes, but by the pressure for action that comes from their members. After all, the miners won their greatest victories in 1972 and 1974 under the leadership of a right wing president, Joe Gormley.

But even when trade union leaders do lead their members in an uncompromising way, as Arthur Scargill did in 1984, they risk the venom and might of the state being hurled against them. The key to victory is not who the leader is—but the self-confidence and self-organisation of the workers and their capacity to win the active support of other workers.

The period of the 1974-79 Labour government is an object lesson in why we can't trust the union leaders. Labour came to power on the back of a huge eruption of working class militancy. But with the TUC's collaboration Labour was able to do what the Tories couldn't—weaken rank and file union power, drive up unemployment and cut real wages for the first time in a generation.

And it was the left wing leaders who were most culpable. Jack Jones, leader of the Transport and General Workers' Union, and Hugh Scanlon, president of the AUEW engineering union, were the two most powerful left leaders. Popular and respected among activists, the Tory press called them "the terrible twins". Yet they were the key architects of the "social contract", and their left reputation convinced a powerful shop stewards movement to go along with it.

None of this means that the divisions within the trade union bureaucracy are irrelevant. There are important differences between right and left wing union leaders and socialists should support the trade union left in its struggles with the right. However, this is different from relying on any official, whatever his or her politics. Workers have to win their own battles, by organising themselves, uniting their forces and taking on the fight.

The fundamental divide in the trade unions is not between right and left wing officials but between the rank and file and the bureaucracy. The only left wing official who will fight in a consistent and determined fashion is one who is accountable to rank and file activists organised outside the confines of the bureaucracy.

The task of socialists is to increase the strength and confidence of the rank and file in relation to the bosses and the state and that requires two things—independence of action in relation to the trade union bureaucracy and political independence from the Labour Party loyalties of the trade union leaders.

The relationship between the rank and file and the trade union bureaucracy is best summed up by the leaders of the first ever shop stewards movement—the Clyde Workers' Committee declaration of November 1915: "We will support the officials just so long as they rightly represent the workers, but we will act independently immediately they misrepresent them."

It remains the definitive statement of rank and file trade unionism—and during the First World War it was no idle boast. To act independently meant preparation in advance. It meant building up networks of activists rooted in the workplaces, who had won the trust of their workmates.

Every week the committee drew together 300 elected representatives from every major factory on Clydeside. As its founding statement continued, "Being composed of delegates from every shop and untrammelled by obsolete rule or law, we claim to represent the true feelings of the workers. We can act immediately according to the merits of the case and the desire of the rank and file."

Effective organisation is based on accountability—democracy from below. It means a number of things: the maximum involvement of everyone in the action; the sense that the rank and file are in control of what is happening and that the leaders are accountable to them; and recognition that solidarity is the key to victory.

The mass strikes of the 1970s that destroyed the Tory government were based on these ideas. Today we are witnessing small but significant moves among workers to create organisation based on the same principles. To be successful rank and file organisation will have to be built around socialist politics.

Leadership, politics and preparation

The pressure the system already exerts on working people—whether they manufacture cars or scan groceries at the supermarket—is going to intensify. The sheer scale of the bosses' onslaught is going to cause some group of workers—we don't know exactly who, where or when—to take centre stage like the teamsters in the coal yards of Minneapolis in 1934, the aerospace workers at Nantes in May 1968, the Glasgow shipyard workers in 1971, or the Asian women working for Gate Gourmet at Heathrow Airport in 2005.

When new groups move into action two things can happen: they discover a power they never knew they had, and they inspire other groups to follow their lead. This can open up a period of rising struggle and political crisis for the ruling class. What happens thereafter depends on the presence and intervention of organised revolutionary socialists in specific struggles and across the movement.

None of this happens automatically. Acts that appear to explode out of the blue are invariably the result of painstaking, and sometimes painful, argument and preparation by individuals.

For example, the decision to occupy Fisher Bendix on Merseyside in 1971 was ratified at a mass meeting of all workers. But the act of occupation was planned and initiated by a group of shop stewards and activists—including a handful of socialists—who'd been inspired by the UCS work-in but had enough political understanding and determination to go for a full-blown occupation.

In the US in the mid-1930s socialists organised and led the key struggles that transformed the balance of power between capital and labour. The Minneapolis teamsters' battle in 1934 is a textbook example of how even a small group of socialists, organised in advance and rooted in the movement, could lead victorious struggles.

Genora Dollinger, a key participant in the great Flint sit-down strike, was always at pains to explain the key role of socialists and Communists in preparing and directing that struggle. In her interviews she stresses how local party meetings on history and socialist theory before the strikes helped produce leaders for the struggle itself; and how all the preparation and discussion, done in advance or in the quieter moments, mattered.

This is not to deny spontaneity, creativity or the unexpected—but to prove that organisation and politics are paramount to success and that it matters what politics win out in the struggle.

In the 1930s the American Communist Party played a great role in the lead up to the sit-downs and in the early breakthroughs that were made. There is no doubting the energy, commitment and sheer courage of its workplace militants and organisers. But its Stalinist politics stymied the creation of a workers' party when the struggle was at its height in 1936 and 1937. The Trotskyists who led the Minneapolis battles and later helped form the American Socialist Workers Party had better politics, but their organisation was too small.

In all the great explosions of struggle set out here, the possibilities and the problems are clear for all to see. In the process of mass political and industrial struggle the working class moves from "a class in itself" to become "a class for itself". Who can deny that it has the capacity to run society after reading only a little of its hidden history?

But it is also pretty clear that the working class needs decisive, independent leadership from within its own ranks if it is to win. For if decisive leadership is not forthcoming then indecisive leadership will be, and instead of spreading and generalising the struggle, the indecisive will look to end it through a deal that gets them off the hook—as the Communist and CGT union leaders did when they rushed to accept the electoral way out of the crisis in May 1968, even when this meant breathing life into General de Gaulle and a frightened French ruling class.

Political clarity is decisive. In 1980 sporadic strikes swept Poland's cities in protest at soaring food prices. They rapidly developed into the biggest workers' revolt seen anywhere in Europe since the strike movement that rocked France in 1968. Their focal point was the huge Lenin shipyards in Gdansk on the Baltic coast, where 16,000 workers went on strike, threw out their state capitalist bosses and began a 17-day occupation.

An eyewitness account from Ewa Barker and Ralph Darlington explains the significance of these events:

> The strike was to develop into a full-blown occupation of the shipyards, which were to be used as the centre for the organisation of no less than 500 workplaces throughout the Baltic region. The result was the creation of the inter-factory committee uniting all the striking enterprises of Gdansk, Gydnia and Sopot.

This led on to the formation of Solidarnosc, the independent Polish trade union. Launched by a conference of delegates from over 3,000 workplaces and claiming 10 million members, it became the focus for everyone who wanted rid of the brutal dictatorship that ruled Poland. The Polish state saw it as a threat to its very existence.

Unfortunately the leaders of Solidarnosc did not understand this. They made the grave mistake of thinking that they could get real change without overthrowing the government, and were naive enough to believe that if Solidarnosc promised not to threaten the state, the state would tolerate the movement.

Shortly before Christmas 1981 the military declared martial law, arrested the entire leadership of Solidarnosc and used heavily armed troops to crush workers' resistance.

A new period of class struggle

The most important lesson from all past struggles is that political argument, political organisation and political leadership are decisive at every level. Success and failure hinge on what socialists are able to do and say and the extent to which key political arguments are made and won.

These arguments are not about past history. They apply very much to the present. We are in a race against time and we urgently need more organised socialists active in every workplace and union branch, in every college and on every street.

In this new period of class struggle there is no such thing as pure spontaneity. As SWP industrial organiser Charlie Kimber pointed out in *Socialist Review* (September 2009):

> Socialists, determined union activists and other radicals kicked off the Waterford and Belfast occupations. A handful of union reps detonated the Enfield resistance, and it might have died within 24 hours if socialists had not delivered instant solidarity. The victory at Linamar in Swansea, where the union convenor was reinstated after an unofficial walkout and an unofficial strike vote, would not have been won without the leadership of socialist activist Rob Williams.
>
> The strikes at the Lindsey Oil Refinery would not have spread to over 20 other sites without the conscious organisation by people on the ground. And the strikes would not have generated the unity needed to win had socialists and others not sidelined the "British jobs for British workers"

slogans which were prominent in the first round of disputes. Vestas is an even sharper example. There would have been no occupation without the painstaking planning and discussion over a period of weeks among a small group of Vestas workers—and the work of socialists and environmental activists in boosting the group.

These occupations and strikes have all raised very sharp political questions... The Visteon occupations began as the G20 leaders met in London. As Gordon Brown and the rest droned on about protecting ordinary people from the effects of the recession, a few miles away hundreds of workers were sacked at six minutes notice—with all their guaranteed rights as Ford workers stripped away. Their occupation highlighted the realities of the situation and the possibility of revolt.

Vestas had the broadest political effect of all. It underlined both the emptiness of the government's commitment to combating unemployment and the fact that all talk of "green jobs" to counter climate change means nothing. Capitalism comes first.

The old and the new are both embedded in the present. On the one hand there are fresh lessons from the occupations and illegal strikes; on the other is the unions' slowness to translate the obvious mood to fight at plants such as Corus and Johnnie Walker into effective resistance... The outcome is not pre-ordained. Everywhere there is a political battle taking place and its outcome will determine whether the working class pays for this crisis.

The impact of the global crisis, the contempt for mainstream politicians and the deep anti-war mood is going to sharpen class struggle, especially but not only among young workers, women workers and immigrant workers.

In that context strikes and occupations can provide the focus for all the accumulated bitterness in society—

the housing crisis, the long wars in Iraq and Afghanistan, corporate greed, corruption in parliament, privatisation, erosion of civil liberties, and 101 other iniquities that people face.

The initial effect of soaring unemployment panicked the union leaders and made many workers doubt their ability to fight. Now a series of successful disputes has raised the tempo and changed the atmosphere of the class struggle in Britain.

The shift that has already taken place is important, but it needs to be developed much further. That means supporting every fight that takes place, spreading solidarity and shaping the resistance.

The occupations have highlighted the possibility of revolt. Just like in the early 1970s when the Upper Clyde work-in triggered over 200 occupations and turned the tide against a vicious Tory government, the successful struggles of today could suddenly become contagious.

The stakes are much higher now and the world is more dangerous and unstable. But after 30 years of defeat and aborted struggle, rank and file initiative is delivering success and offers real hope of bigger victories to come.

Socialism and workers' control

We celebrate every advance, be it a wage rise or the saving of jobs, but we also recognise that these are steps on the way to a deeper change, the construction of a socialist society based on genuine workers' democracy, where power rests with those who produce society's wealth. In that sense workers' actions—and strikes and occupations in particular—are living proof that workers do have the power to change the world.

Unfortunately socialism has been identified, especially by its enemies, with state ownership and bureaucratic control. This is particularly the case with those who used to call countries like the former Soviet Union or Poland "socialist" simply because their economies were nationalised and despite the fact that they had not a shred of workers' democracy.

The reformist tradition sees socialism as something that comes from above, to be achieved on workers' behalf by their "leaders". Apart from voting at election time, workers are expected to play a passive role, looking on while their elected leaders transform society for them.

In May 1936 an alliance that included the French Socialist and Communist parties won the general election and French workers responded with a wave of factory occupations through which they sought to translate their electoral victory into economic and social gains.

In the process they threatened the very basis of the capitalist order and their Communist and Socialist "leaders" rushed to get them back to work, opening the door for the right to regain control and then launch its counter-attack on the working class movement.

The standard right wing view of revolution is a conspiracy engineered by an elite with the mass of people as passive bystanders. The authentic Marxist view is very different, here voiced by Trotsky:

> The most indubitable feature of a revolution is the direct interference of the masses in historic events...a revolution is first of all the forcible entrance of the masses into the realm of rulership over their own destiny.

The SWP stands in the tradition of socialism based on genuine democracy and workers' control—socialism from below. Only workers can liberate themselves—no one can do it for them. The role of a revolutionary socialist workers' party is not to lecture but to learn from the workers in struggle and to teach them in struggle.

During the 1905 Revolution, the Russian revolutionary Lenin wrote:

> When the social reformists talk about "the education of the masses", they usually mean something schoolmasterly, pedantic, something that demoralises the masses and instils in them bourgeois prejudice. The real education of the masses can never be separated from their independent political and especially revolutionary struggle. Only struggle educates the exploited class. Only struggle discloses to it the magnitude of its own power, widens its horizon, enhances its abilities, clarifies its mind and forges its will.

The working class is the only social force in society that has the potential to challenge capitalism and bring about lasting change. Under capitalism workers' control can only go so far. If workers take over their factory and nothing else changes, they can eventually end up competing on the market and organising their own exploitation.

Genuine workers' control can only exist in the framework of a democratically planned society in which people discuss and decide the overall targets and priorities. On taking power in 1917 the Russian workers' government passed a decree confirming workers' control. But the real movement had come from below. Workers had no option but to take over the workplaces and run them for themselves.

John Reed, a US socialist in Russia during the very early days of the revolution, described the process in his *Ten Days that Shook the World*:

> There was a committee meeting in one of the factories, where a workman rose and said, "Comrades, why do we worry? The question of technical experts is not a difficult one. Remember, the boss wasn't a technical expert; the

boss didn't know engineering or chemistry or book keeping. All he did was to own. When he wanted technical help he hired men to do it for him. Well, now we are the boss. Let's hire engineers, book-keepers and so forth—to work for us."

USEFUL BOOKS AND ARTICLES

Those marked [OP] are out of print, but can be found second hand.

Chris Harman, *A People's History of the World* (Verso, 2008)
Paul Mason, *Live Working or Die Fighting: How the Working Class Went Global* (Harvill Secker, 2007)

On Italy:
Antonio Gramsci, *Selections from Political Writings, 1910-20* (Central, 2003)
Paolo Spriano, *The Occupation of the Factories* (Pluto, 1975) [OP]
Gwyn Williams, *Proletarian Order: Antonio Gramsci, Factory Councils and the Origins of Communism in Italy 1911-21* (Pluto, 1975) [OP]

On France 1936:
Jacques Danos and Marcel Gibelin, *June '36: Class Struggle and the Popular Front in France* (Bookmarks, 1986) [OP]
Leon Trotsky, *Whither France?* (1936), is available at www.marxists.org/archive/trotsky/1936/whitherfrance/index.htm

On the US:
Farrell Dobbs, *Teamster Rebellion* (Pathfinder, 2004)
John Newsinger, "1934: The Year of the Fightback" in *International Socialism 122* (spring 2009), available at www.isj.org.uk
Art Preis, *Labor's Giant Step: Twenty Years of the CIO* (Pathfinder, 1972) [OP]
Susan Rosenthal, "Genora Dollinger Remembers the 1936-37 General Motors Sit-Down Strike", is available at www.marxists.org/history/etol/newspape/amersocialist/genora.htm
Sharon Smith, *Subterranean Fire: A History of Working Class Radicalism in the USA* (Haymarket, 2006)
Megan Trudell, "The Hidden History of US Radicalism", in *International Socialism 111* (summer 2006), available at www.isj.org.uk

On France 1968:
Chris Harman, *The Fire Last Time: 1968 and After* (Bookmarks, 1998)

On Britain:
Tony Cliff, *In the Thick of Workers' Struggle* (Bookmarks, 2002)
Ralph Darlington and Dave Lyddon, *Glorious Summer: Class Struggle in Britain, 1972* (Bookmarks, 2001)